# MUNCHKIN CATS
# AND THE MUNCHKIN CAT

Your Munchkin Cats Bible:
Includes Munchkin Cats, Teacup Kittens, Munchkin Kittens, Dwarf
Cats, Dwarf Kittens, And Miniature Cats, All Covered!

By Susanne Saben
© DYM Worldwide Publishers

DYM Worldwide Publishers

ISBN: 978-1-911355-00-7

**Published by DYM Worldwide Publishers 2016.**

**Copyright and Trademarks.** This publication is Copyright 2016 by DYM Worldwide Publishers. All products, publications, software, and services mentioned and recommended in this publication are protected by trademarks. In such instance, all trademarks & copyright belonging to the respective owners. All rights reserved. No part of this book may be reproduced or transferred in any form or by any means, graphic, electronic, or mechanical, including but not limited to photocopying, recording, taping, scanning, or by any information storage retrieval system, without the written permission of the author. Pictures used in this book are royalty free pictures purchased from stock photo websites with full rights for use within this work.

**Disclaimer and Legal Notice.** This product is not legal or medical advice and should not be interpreted in that manner. You need to do your own due diligence to determine if the content of this product is right for you. The author, publisher, distributors, and or/affiliates of this product are not liable for any damages or losses associated with the content in this product. While every attempt has been made to verify the information shared in this publication, neither the author, publisher, distributors, and/or affiliates assume any responsibility for errors, omissions, or contrary interpretation of the subject matter herein. Any perceived slights to any specific person(s) or organization(s) are purely unintentional. We have no control over the nature, content, and availability of the websites listed in this book. The inclusion of any website links does not necessarily imply a recommendation or endorse the views expressed within them. DYM Worldwide Publishers takes no responsibility for, and will not be liable for, the websites being temporarily or being removed from the Internet. The accuracy and completeness of the information provided herein and opinions stated herein are not guaranteed or warranted to produce any particular results, and the advice or strategies, contained herein may not be suitable for every individual. The author, publisher, distributors, and/or affiliates shall not be liable for any loss incurred as a consequence of the use and application, directly or indirectly of any information presented in this work. This publication is designed to provide information in regards to the subject matter covered. The information included in this book has been compiled to give an overview of the topics covered. The information contained in this book has been compiled to provide an overview of the subject. It is not intended as medical advice and should not be construed as such. For a firm diagnosis of any medical conditions you should consult a doctor or veterinarian (as related to animal health). The writer, publisher, distributors, and/or affiliates of this work are not responsible for any damages or negative consequences following any of the treatments or methods highlighted in this book. Website links are for informational purposes only and should not be seen as a personal endorsement; the same applies to any products or services mentioned in this work. The reader should also be aware that although the web links included were correct at the time of writing they may become out of date in the future. Any pricing or currency exchange rate information was accurate at the date of writing but may become out of date in the future. The Author,

Publisher, distributors, and/or affiliates assume no responsibility for pricing and currency exchange rates mentioned within this work.

# Table of Contents

\* \* \*

Foreword.................................................................................. 10

**Chapter 1 – An Introduction to Munchkin Cats and Other Miniature Cat Breeds**................................................ 12

**Munchkin Cats, A Quick History** .............................. 14

**Characteristics: Traits and Munchkin Cat Temperament**...... 15

**Potential Health Issues with Munchkin Kittens and Munchkin Cats** ................................................................................ 17

**The Different Kinds of Munchkin Cats** .......................... 18

Standard............................................................................18

Super Short.......................................................................19

Rug Hugger .......................................................................19

The Munchkin Kitty Cousins and Teacup Cats .................20

The Lambkin Cat...............................................................20

The Scottish Fold Munchkin ............................................22

The Persian Munchkin Cat................................................23

Teacup Cats......................................................................24

**Chapter 2 – How Do I Become a Good Munchkin Cat Parent?**........................................................................ 27

**Responsible Munchkin Cat Parenting** ......................... 30

1. Thou shalt understand your munchkin kittens and its lineage...............................................................................30

2. Thou shalt provide your munchkin cat with food, shelter, and affection.........................................................................31

3. Thou shalt train your munchkin cat lovingly. ...............32

4. Thou shalt protect your munchkin cat from harm and from doing harm........................................................................32

5. Thou shalt commit to regular vet checkups and bring your dwarf cat to the vet when it is sick....................................33

6. Thou shalt care for your munchkin cat's health. ..........34

7. Thou shalt make the choice of neutering or spaying your dwarf cat pet. ....................................................................34

8. Thou shalt make sure that your pet has proper identification and papers....................................................................35
9. Thou shalt respect your munchkin cat.........................................35
10. Thou shalt not more abandon your munchkin cat..................36

# Chapter 3 – Where Can I Get a Munchkin Cat?.................... 37
Munchkin Cat Adoption from a Shelter ................................. 37
Finding a Reputable Munchkin Cat Breeder ........................ 40
1. Has too many breeds, or too many munchkin cats, making the spaces too crowded. (Usually with too few workers.) .........41
2. They talk more about titles; doesn't have a lot to say about the individual munchkin kittens' characteristics........................42
3. Only has bad things to say about other munchkin cat breeders. .......................................................................................42
4. Unconcerned about what kind of home you will be providing for the munchkin kittens..................................................................42
5. Charges prices that are much too high for things like the size of the munchkin kittens' body or their color or the color patterns. .....................................................................................43
How to Spot Munchkin Kitten Farms or Kitten Mills ............. 43
Papers and Documents for Your Munchkin Cat ....................... 45

# Chapter 4 – Understanding a Munchkin Cat's Personality and Temperament .............................................................. 48
Munchkin Cats are a Very Friendly Breed............................. 49
Munchkin Cats Are Intelligent ............................................. 51
Munchkin Cats Are Born Explorers....................................... 52
Munchkin Cats Are Well-adjusted and Even-tempered ......... 52
Munchkin Cats Are Low Maintenance ................................... 53

# Chapter 5 – How to Choose the Right Munchkin Cat for You
.................................................................................................. 55
What is the Ideal Pet Munchkin Cat? .................................... 56
Hand-reared or Orphan Cats vs. Litter Munchkin Kittens .... 57
What is the Right Age to Bring a Munchkin Cat Home?.......... 59
Should You Choose an Adult or Kitten Munchkin Cat? .......... 60
Choosing the Munchkin Cat for You ...................................... 63
1. Talk to the breeder or the shelter volunteers.........................63
2. Watch how the munchkin cats or kittens interact with others.
.......................................................................................65
3. See how the munchkin cat or munchkin kitten responds to you.......................................................................................65

4. Assess the munchkin cat's health. ................................66
**Ask if the Munchkin Cat Has Insurance** ........................ **67**
**Be Prepared to Walk Away** ............................................. **68**
**Visit the Munchkin Cats Ahead of Time** ........................ **69**

**Chapter 6 – Preparing Your Home for Your New Munchkin Cat** .................................................................................. **71**
**How to Cat-Proof Your Home for Your New Munchkin Cat** ... **71**
1. Remove all poisonous plants inside and outside your house. ................................................................................72
2. Keep your cleaning supplies in a storage area for this specific purpose. Make sure that the storage area can be closed up. .....73
3. Make sure that all medication is kept in a special medicine kit or cabinet, safely out of reach. ......................................75
4. Unplug appliances that aren't in use or tuck them away, out of reach. .......................................................................76
5. Cords and draperies should be coiled or tied neatly up in a knot. ..............................................................................77
6. Always keep the dryer closed and always check it before closing. ............................................................................77
7. Install switch covers for your disposal switch. Make sure it is closed unless you plan to use it. ..........................................78
8. Make sure your garbage is stored in a lidded container that shuts to keep your munchkin cat out. .........................................78
9. Check for small choking hazards. ...............................79
10. Put away any shiny trinkets like jewelry. ...................79
11. Make sure your shelves are secure. .........................79
12. Secure the screens. ...............................................80
13. Keep the toilet bowl closed. .....................................80
**Building a Home for Your Munchkin Cat** ...................... **81**
1. Litter box. ...............................................................82
2. Dishes. ..................................................................83
3. Scratching post .......................................................84
**Your Munchkin Cat's First Night** ................................. **85**

**Chapter 7 – Feeding Your New Munchkin Cat** ................ **87**
**What is the Best Diet for Your Munchkin Cat?** ............... **88**
**Is Wet Food or Dry Food Better for Your Munchkin Cat?** ....... **88**
**How Often Should You Feed Your Munchkin Cat?** ............ **89**
**How to Choose the Right Cat Food For Your Munchkin Cat** ... **90**
**The Common Mistakes Cat Parents Make When Feeding**

**Munchkin Cats** ....................................................... **92**
1. Feeding the munchkin cat too much..............................93
2. Giving the munchkin cat food that has too many
carbohydrates. ...................................................93
3. Feeding munchkin cats food that is bad for cats. ...............93
4. Feeding the munchkin cat only dry food or not offering
enough water...................................................94
5. Unknowingly encouraging nutritional deficiencies. ............95
6. Cat Treats and Your Munchkin Cat...........................95

**Chapter 8 – Caring for Your Munchkin Cat and
Understanding Its Needs** ......................................... **96**
Grooming Your Munchkin Cat ......................................... **98**
Giving Your Munchkin Cat Proper Health Care and
Maintenance ............................................................ **103**
When Should You Bring Your Munchkin Cat to the Vet ....... **106**

**Chapter 9 – Can You Train A Munchkin Cat?**..................... **107**
Teach Your Munchkin Cat to Sit On Command ..................... **108**
Teach Your Munchkin Cat to Come on Command................. **110**
How to Train Your Munchkin Cat to Use the Toilet.............. **110**
Use Treats and Training to Reinforce Good Behavior ......... **112**

**Chapter 10 – Munchkin Cat Groups, and Other Fun
Activities** .............................................................. **113**
Try Going on a Munchkin Cat Vacation ......................... **115**
1. The Queen Mary 2 ..........................................116
2. The Kimpton Hotels.........................................116
3. Hotel Monteleone in New Orleans............................116

**Chapter 11 – Living Happily with Your Munchkin Cat**....**118**
1. Walk your cat on a leash. ..................................... **119**
2. Get some toys. ................................................. **120**
3. Offer perches by the windows. ............................... **120**
4. Put cat grass around the house. ............................. **121**
5. Buy or build a cat tree. ...................................... **121**
6. Buy a cat bed. ................................................. **122**
Final Thoughts on Your Journey with Your Munchkin Cat. **123**

# Foreword

\* \* \*

These days, pets – especially cats – have become members of the family, as cared for and as beloved as a child; and why shouldn't they be? Cats bring joy to the family in many different ways, and they bring distinct personalities that make them just as real to interact with as a friend and family member. But unlike people, cats are dependent on us for their basic needs, to be taught the rules, and to understand the living environment that is your home. As cat owners, we have the responsibility to understand our cats and to offer attention, affection, and care as well as boundaries to keep them safe and content.

When we care for our cats properly, we have the potential to create a strong and lasting bond that can be genuinely rewarding to all parties. Cats, especially munchkin cats, can grow to become an important and valuable part of our family and our lives. But if we let them down by treating them as fixtures in our home, we are creating a problem for ourselves and abusing a pet that is unable to protect itself or fend for itself.

If you are looking to add a new cat to your family, then munchkin cats are the perfect choice. Smaller than most cats, it gives the appearance of being permanently youthful and its temperament supports this completely. Extroverted, energetic, and fun loving, munchkins are bound to be constantly the center of attention and the life of every party. They will be there to greet you enthusiastically at every end of the day, eager to play with you as well as other members of the family – including other cats and dogs.

Understanding your munchkin cat is the first step to becoming a responsible and loving parent and master to your new pet which is exactly what we want to offer in this book. Meant for long-time munchkin cat lovers and new munchkin owners alike, your Munchkin Cat Bible acts as a quick reference as well as a comprehensive guide and a fun read for like-minded cat lovers who want to get to know their munchkins better.

Your Munchkin Cat Bible takes you through owning and loving your munchkin cat, from finding the right munchkin cat or munchkin kitten for you to taking steps to having a well-behaved and responsive pet, to finding new ways to spend time and have fun with your munchkin. Buying this book will help you become the responsible and informed parent and owner that every munchkin cat deserves.

# Chapter 1 – An Introduction to Munchkin Cats and Other Miniature Cat Breeds

\* \* \*

Welcome to Munchkin Cats and the Munchkin Cat, a book written for all munchkin parents and potential munchkin parents who are looking for a comprehensive and easy-to-use book. Congratulations, you've found it! This book covers the different stages of munchkin ownership. Whether you're looking to adopt a munchkin cat, to get to know your new dwarf cat more, to find common ground with a munchkin cat that has developed problems fitting in, or to look for more fun things to do with your munchkin kittens, this book has something for you.

One of the reasons why I wrote this book is to help set the expectations of would-be owners and to avoid what I would call 'mistaken adoptions.' Like any parent, potential munchkin kitten owners have the responsibility to know what they're getting into. Sometimes, we fall in love with a munchkin cat, and we take one home without knowing what adoption actually asks of us. These are the munchkin cats that end up in shelters because people underestimated the demand of having a cat as a member of their family.

When we're taking home a cute munchkin cat, we never imagine that we would ever want to drop it off at a shelter a few months later. What every cat owner wants is a loving and well-mannered companion, a pet that offers nurturing and accepts it at the same time; and that's what we want every munchkin owner to achieve with this book, by becoming a well-informed cat parent.

Every cat owner gets the cat he or she deserves which is a way of saying that our pets reflect our handling of them. With this book, I hope to help you gain an improved understanding of your munchkin cat, determine whether a munchkin is a good fit for you and your family, and help you have a great time and a loving life with your munchkin pet.

*Figure 1: The Munchkin Cat is a Very Inquisitive Creature, as You'll Soon Find Out!*

Munchkin Cat Fast Facts!
Height:                               7 to 8 inches standard or about
                                      18 to 20 centimeters

| | |
|---|---|
| Weight: | 5 to 9 pounds or about 2 to 4 kilograms |
| Lifespan: | 12 to 14 years |
| Physique: | Small, short legs; normal-sized body |
| Best suited for: | Families with children or single people |
| Temperament: | Playful and active |

## Munchkin Cats, A Quick History

You may be surprised to know that our short-legged cat friends are relatively very young in terms of cat breeds. Unlike Persian cats (documented as early as the 1600s in Italy) and Siamese cats (illustrated in manuscripts from way back in 1350 AD, yikes), our munchkin cats today can be traced back to a pregnant cat in 1983 found in Louisiana by a music teacher named Sandra Hochenedel after it was chased by a bulldog. Hochenedel took the cat in and named her Blackberry.

Blackberry gave birth to a healthy litter, with half of the kittens born short-legged. Hochenedel gave a male, short-legged kitten to a friend, Kay LaFrance, who named the kitten Toulouse. Toulouse and Blackberry eventually parented more short-legged munchkin kittens and became the ancestors of the munchkin cats that we have today.

Did you know?

Munchkin cats were named after the munchkins in the novel The

Wizard of Oz. Another more official name for them is Louisiana Creole Cats.

Despite its humble beginnings, munchkin cats gained in popularity when they were featured on the front page of the Wall Street Journal in 1995. The article described munchkins as a polarizing breed that had cat communities in an uproar over deciding whether its short stature was a deformity or an acceptable trait. In the end, the munchkins won out, gaining acceptance as an official cat breed and as beloved pets in homes all over the world.

## Characteristics: Traits and Munchkin Cat Temperament

The most distinctive and obvious traits for munchkins are their small stature. As adorably short-legged as the dachshund and the basset hound dog breeds, munchkin cats are easily recognizable for their shortness that also gives them a longer and slinkier appearance. As a matter of fact, this cute cat breed shares the same genetic mutation as short-legged dogs but without most of the health problems that come with it for canines.

Did you know?

Munchkin cats and munchkin kittens can be hoarders. They love shiny things and will hide the ones that they find like small treasures, to play with later. That's how they earned the nickname magpies.

*Figure 2: The short characteristic stature of the Munchkin Cat gives it a very unique look.*

Other than its short legs, munchkin cats are distinguished by their regular body size as adults, with a weight range of 5 to 9 pounds or 2 to 4 kilograms. The coat can be long or short and comes in just about any pattern, color, or patina that you can imagine on any cat!

As a pet, a munchkin's temperament is also ideal because of its innate friendliness and playfulness. Known for being energetic and extroverted, this short-legged cat will always be willing to play and will get along well with other members of the family, especially children, other cats, and friendly dogs.

They make for loving, affectionate, and sociable pets and would make a great addition to any family.

## Potential Health Issues with Munchkin Kittens and Munchkin Cats

Unlike short-legged dog breeds that suffer from a range of spinal problems, munchkin cats are free of any health problems for the most part. Their mobility and movement aren't stunted by their size and build. If anything, they seem to enjoy more agility, thanks to cats' inherent flexibility and a stable center of gravity that they get from being closer to the ground. If you see a munchkin cat run and play, you'll notice that they're much faster than regular sized cats.

However, munchkins are prone to a health problem called lordosis because of its stature. Lordosis is a dip in the spine along the shoulder blades that can lead to difficulty in breathing and cardiac distress in more severe cases. In a worst case scenario, lordosis can be lethal to a munchkin cat.

Lordosis actually occurs naturally in cats and in most female mammals when they are mating. Their spine arcs downward, creating a constriction that can lead to similar symptoms as the munchkin but in a much lighter and less dangerous sense. In the munchkin cat, however, the downward arc of lordosis is permanent and can become more aggressive as they age.

Responsible breeders work hard to make sure that their kittens avoid the genetic disposition that leads to munchkin cat health problems, but lordosis still occurs today; that's the bad news. The good news is that lordosis is easily spotted early in the life of any cat breed during the kitten stage which means that the chances of you taking home a cat with lordosis is very slim.

Munchkin kittens with lordosis will display a swayback and a potbelly that is much larger than normal. They usually do not live beyond 12 weeks after birth. If they make it beyond the 12-week mark with lordosis, the risk that it presents will be significantly decreased.

A lot of munchkin kittens are also born with back feet that curl backward. Don't despair! This is a normal trait among munchkins and won't cause any munchkin cat health problems or difficulties for your beloved pet.

**The Different Kinds of Munchkin Cats**

There are different kinds of munchkin cats out there, specifically three types based on the length of their legs. These different types are:

*Standard*

The standard munchkin kitty is your regular short-legged munchkin with legs that are about half the length of a regular cat's legs.

When you come across munchkin kittens that are described as non-standard, it means that the kitten came from a munchkin litter but has legs that are normal in length. They basically look like your regular cat but still have the munchkin short-legged cat gene in them.

### Super Short

Munchkins described as super short have legs that are even shorter than your standard munchkin cats! With legs less than 1/2 of the length of a regular cat, your super short munchkin will display even more emphasis on body length, with characteristics closer to a dachshund as compared to a basset hound.

*Figure 3: An example of a Super Short Munchkin Cat.*

### Rug Hugger

A rug hugger munchkin cat has legs so short that its belly is practically touching the floor. Be careful when getting out of bed when you've got a rug hugger on the lose; you just might accidentally step on your dwarf cat! Possibly the cutest of the bunch, rug huggers are prized by munchkin lovers everywhere.

## The Munchkin Kitty Cousins and Teacup Cats

It's no secret why dwarf kittens are so popular and well-loved all over the globe; they're cute, they're cuddly, and they're like miniature cats! Really, what's not to love? The great thing about munchkin cats, in particular, is that they're not only short-legged and therefore cuter than your average, garden variety cat; they are also fun loving, affectionate, extroverted, and intelligent. You know what could be even better? Cats that are part munchkin while also having the traits of other favorite breeds!

While dwarf cats are not as widely accepted in cat associations outside of the United States, they are still welcome in just about all cat lovers' homes and they are certainly adored inside the US. The resistance to dwarf cats is partly because of the breeding practices and its risks. When munchkins are bred with each other, extra care has to be taken, or there will be a lot of fatalities in the litter. However, by breeding munchkin cats with a normal sized cat, you can have a more normal mortality rate and get a beautiful crossbreed cat too.

## The Lambkin Cat

There are munchkin cats, there are teacup kittens, and then there are... Lambkins? The Lambkin cat is a cross between the Selkirk Rex and a munchkin cat. The Selkirk Rex is known for its distinctly curly hair. Everything about this breed of cats is curly - even its whiskers! And when you cross the Selkirk Rex and the munchkin cat, you get an adorable curly, short-legged cat. But it's more than just looks that make this combination of two breeds a real keeper.

Like the munchkin cat, the Selkirk Rex isn't the type to get aggressive. It is a cat breed that generally stays calm, cool, and collected. And even though it is less playful and less energetic than our munchkin breed, the Selkirk Rex gets along well with people and fit right into a family, whether there's just one person, or a couple, or kids. When you cross the two breeds together, you get the Lambkin – a short-legged cat that brings out the best in both breeds.

Like the Selkirk Rex and the munchkin cat, the Lambkin comes in a wide range of coat colors. They are only distinguished by the shortness of their legs and their very curly hair. Also like the Selkirk, the Lambkin will have all three layers of a cat's coat. Add the curliness of the hair and you'll understand why a Lambkin will need more brushing and grooming than a regular munchkin cat.

A Lambkin's coat does have a tendency towards oiliness and will need to be brushed and groomed a lot more than a munchkin cat. And while most cat parents will rarely have to bathe their munchkin, a Lambkin will have to be bathed more regularly. It's the kind of cat that's more high maintenance than what most cat parents are used to. But don't worry; it's affectionate and playful nature will make the added effort worth it.

The Lambkin does have added health issues that other dwarf kittens will lack, something that it gets from the Selkirk Rex breed. It is at risk for kidney problems and eye infection. Be sure to keep an eye out for these problems and to see the vet regularly for checkups.

### The Scottish Fold Munchkin

One of the more popular cross-bred dwarf cat is the Scottish fold munchkin. Also called Scottish kilts, these cats display the same characteristics as a Scottish fold with a 50% chance of getting folded ears, while also displaying the dwarfish characteristics of a short-legged munchkin cat.

*Figure 4: A playful Scottish Fold Munchkin looking very alert!*

Did you know?

Scottish folds are also known as Highland folds, Scottish fold longhair, Longhair fold, and Coupari.

This particular crossbreed is beloved by many and is sought after by plenty of cat lovers because of the Scottish fold cat's already quirky looks. The folded ears give these cats an owlish look that is easily distinguishable from other breeds. Pair that with this breed's unusually loving and affectionate nature, and the cuteness of a dwarf cat and you get a highly prized feline pet.

Note that all Scottish fold kittens are born with straight ears. The ears fold after about 21 days, a trait that also applies to Scottish fold munchkins. The kittens with ears that stay straight even after the time period are aptly called straights.

Munchkins and Scottish folds produce kittens that make ideal pets given the natures of both breeds. Scottish folds tend to be placid, good-natured, and well-adjusted cats. Match these traits with a munchkin's fun loving, intelligent, and affectionate nature and you get an ideal household pet.

### The Persian Munchkin Cat

With the intense following that dwarf cats and dwarf kittens have today, it's no surprise that one of the most popular and sought after crossbreeds is that of a munchkin cat and a Persian cat.

The Persian cat is the most popular breed of cat in the United States and with good reason. Its long, luxurious hair and its sheen is adored by most cat lovers. Its nature - a regal aloofness while also being naturally placid and easy going - make the Persian an ideal companion, even when living in small spaces.

Persian cats also have naturally short legs, making the cross between Persians and munchkins almost a no-brainer. Today, the Persian munchkin cat has become so well established that it has earned its own nickname - the Minuet.

The Minuet has inherited the munchkin cat's short legs while also displaying the Persian cat's dense coat, substantial boning, and natural beauty. This crossbreed is highly prized among cat lovers and is one of the most easily distinguishable cats in the world.

### Teacup Cats

One of the most common questions asked about a dwarf cat is the difference between a teacup cat and a munchkin. Are those two names to describe the same cat? Is a munchkin cat a teacup cat and vice versa?

In fact, munchkins and teacup cats are completely different (but are just as cute and adorable and smallish in size). Munchkin cats are marked by short legs, which means that their bodies are similar to that of regular cats, but their legs are short, giving them the build similar to a dachshund dog – short, but long. Teacup cats and kittens, on the other hand, are simply smaller versions of a regular size cat. In general, teacup cats can be easily recognized by their size and weight as adults. While regular-sized cats' sizes and weights can range between 11 to 14 pounds or 4 to 6 kilograms for females and a little more for males, cats that qualify as teacup, dwarf, or midget would weigh as little as 3 to 6 pounds or 1 to 2 kilograms for females and 3 to 6.5 pounds or 1 to almost 3 kilograms for males. At the University of Melbourne School of Veterinary Science in 1979, an adult dwarf cat was found that weighed as little as 2 pounds or a little under 2 kilograms.

Teacup cats are smaller in every way than regular cats, a result that may be caused by a variety of reasons: some genetic, some hormonal, and some even environmental. A true teacup cat, however, is smaller in stature because of a genetic dwarfism that makes it a proportionally miniature cat. It is simply a regular cat that will never achieve full growth.

*Figure 5: A teacup cat can be cute but can also have health problems so be aware when selecting one.*
These cats are just as adorable and in need of love as any

other cat. However, they are not a real cat breed and are generally cats that are unfortunately considered the runt of the litter - kittens that, for one reason or another, will not grow to full size. This also means that most teacup kittens will be plagued with health problems and are much more vulnerable than regular sized cats. Be extra cautious when bringing home a teacup cat and be prepared to meet its irregular needs.

That being said, teacup cats and teacup kittens need care, attention, and family just like any other pet.

## Chapter 2 – How Do I Become a Good Munchkin Cat Parent?

\* \* \*

So, you're seriously considering bringing home a munchkin kitten or maybe you're still toying with the idea. Perhaps you have friends who have dwarf kittens, and you adore playing with their pets, or maybe you had a cat before and want a new one to add to your family now. Regardless, you already have one foot in the door of cat parenthood, and you're ready to take the next step. The big question is, are you prepared to become a munchkin parent?

*Figure 6: Munchkin Cats need attention and love, and remember it's a time commitment – but a rewarding one!*

| Munchkin Cat Pros | Munchkin Cat Cons |
| --- | --- |
| They are fun to play with – especially munchkin cats! | You will need to clean out the litter box. |
| They are very cute and interactive. | Their claws are sharp (but you can clip them). |
| They come with their own set of unique personalities. | They are willful and have a mind of their own. |
| They are intelligent and require very little training (think potty training). | They have predatory instincts and will present you with dead mice (they will then expect to be praised). |
| They require less exercise (compared to dogs). | They will shed. |
| They keep themselves clean and are low maintenance in general. | You will need to take them to visit the vet regularly. |
| They offer pest control. | You will need to make sure that they are fed every day. |
| They are typically happy indoors and don't need a lot of space. | You will need to care for them - and plan vacations around them. |
| They purr :) | |

As someone who has parented and loved cats all my life, I can tell you that it can be a very rewarding and loving experience. My cats are part of my family, and they are a constant source of joy and affection for me, my special someone, and eventually with our kids as well. They can make home life interesting and fun! On the other hand, having cats - whether full-sized or dwarf kittens - comes with its own particular set of responsibilities.

Just to be responsible regarding cat adoption, let's take a look at the pros and cons of having a cat in the family.

That is about as honest a pros and cons list as I can make. I have loved plenty of cats before, and I love the cats that I have now; but even as an experienced cat parent, I still have those days when I am feeling too tired to take them to the vet when I have told myself I would. Going on vacations are also always a logistical challenge, from who takes care of the house to who takes care of the cats. Finding sitters isn't as straightforward as many would think because most cats will have peculiar habits (the same way people do). One of my cats will not eat wet cat food while the other can't seem to stand the dry ones. Such is the life of a cat parent.

*Figure 7: A Munchkin Cat in a classic hunting pose.*

But then again, it is always worth it to have cats in my home every day, all the time. I have a munchkin cat in the family right now, and she is an endless source of amusement and affection for everyone. Munchkins are especially adorable because of their innate playfulness and friendliness. While some cat breeds are known for being aloof and regal, munchkins are the exact opposite. They will romp and play and entertain, and they won't hold back or discriminate when it comes to showing affection. They will be best friends with the entire family, even with dogs!

**Responsible Munchkin Cat Parenting**

Just like becoming actual parents, welcoming a munchkin cat (or any pet) to your home comes with a set of responsibilities. To make things really simple, I've put together the 10 commandments of being a responsible munchkin parent:

*1. Thou shalt understand your munchkin kittens and its lineage.*

Whether you're buying a pet munchkin or adopting from a local shelter, part of your responsibility is to ask questions about your cat. Considering the degree of cuteness a munchkin cat has, your soon-to-be pet probably has your undivided attention. Try to break free for a few minutes and get to know the rest of the litter, the other munchkin kittens. Try to see how well they respond to your presence. Do they shy away scared? Or are they willing to play with you and welcome your touch? How the rest of the litter acts can be a good way of gauging how socialized your munchkin may be.

Ask about the parents too, including any health problems they may have experienced. All this is just a good way to better prepare yourself for anything that may happen down the road. It doesn't hurt to be prepared and well informed.

**2. *Thou shalt provide your munchkin cat with food, shelter, and affection.***

This goes almost without saying.

A major part of your responsibilities as a munchkin cat parent is to provide food, shelter, and other basic needs to your little munchkin cat; and this includes affection and attention. Cats are social beings and will look to you for interaction and love. These requirements are part of what keeps them healthy and stable and good pets.

Providing food and shelter are easy needs to meet, for the most part, but do make arrangements during those times when you can't be around to take care of them, especially during vacations. Find someone to check in on them, to make sure they're fed and healthy, and to interact with them a little. Simply put, make arrangements for them when you leave your home for longer than a day.

### 3. *Thou shalt train your munchkin cat lovingly.*

Munchkin cats and kittens are adorable, playful, and social creatures. They can feel negative human interactions and are capable of responding in kind. Avoid raising an ill-tempered pet by steering clear of any abusive training methods. For example, do not under any circumstances try to discipline your pet munchkin by hitting it or by inflicting any form of physical pain. Not only will the lesson be completely lost, but you will also be creating behavioral problems that could get worse over time. You want a cat that understands the rules and abides by them; not one that is afraid of you, or is insecure, and possibly unstable.

Another form of abusive discipline is keeping your munchkin cat or munchkin kitten locked up in small spaces when it has misbehaved. Instead of applying negative pressure, you can discourage bad behavior by encouraging and rewarding good behavior.

### 4. *Thou shalt protect your munchkin cat from harm and from doing harm.*

Sometimes, when a cat gets in trouble - with the neighbors or with the neighbors' pets - we are too quick to punish them even if their behavior likely stems from how they are treated and raised. From experience, I find that a well-treated cat, dwarf cat or otherwise, does not inflict harm on others. By taking the time to give our pets basic training and by setting clear boundaries, we are protecting them not just from causing harm but also from being harmed. Also, having cat enclosures that keep them from wandering into areas that are potentially dangerous for them can go a long way in feline safety.

**5. Thou shalt commit to regular vet checkups and bring your dwarf cat to the vet when it is sick.**

*Figure 8: Munchkin Cat health is not too much of a challenge if you have a good vet.*

I cannot stress the importance of trips to the vet enough. Get your munchkin cat proper shots, make sure that it is protected from diseases!

After you take home your munchkin, be sure to take it to the vet as well. The vet will help you with the shots that your pet needs, the papers that need to be drawn up, the visits that you will need to make and how often. This is a financial commitment that all pet owners have to make. It is necessary for your munchkin cat health as well as the health and protection of other family members that share the house.

## 6. *Thou shalt care for your munchkin cat's health.*

Isn't this commandment the same as the fifth one? Not exactly.

This is less about going to the vet and more about understanding your munchkin and keeping an eye out for trouble. Is the munchkin acting more docile than usual? Has it not eaten for the entire day? Is it exhibiting signs of sickness or weakness? Caring about your cat's health and well-being is essential to being a good cat parent.

Also, keep yourself informed in terms of your munchkin cat's possible health issues. A little light reading and research will help you avoid any bandwagon trends that may create more problems than solve them.

## 7. *Thou shalt make the choice of neutering or spaying your dwarf cat pet.*

Unless you are a professional cat breeder, I would strongly advise you to either have your munchkin neutered or spayed (depending on the gender). Breeding munchkin cats require knowledge and study that most average cat owners do not have at their disposal. Breeding will also require more special attention, health training, and just more financial commitment in general. If you are unable to create a safe environment for your munchkins to breed, then take the trip to the vet and avoid any grief.

There are plenty of risks to breeding munchkin cats and will be explored more thoroughly in a later chapter.

*8. Thou shalt make sure that your pet has proper identification and papers.*

Make your adoption official!

This is basically part of bringing your munchkin cat home or taking it to the vet but don't overlook the official papers that make your munchkin truly yours. Don't forget; without these documents, you won't be able to travel with your pet.

If you are so inclined, you can also get pet passports under the Pet Travel Scheme. You can also invest in microchipping so that you never lose your beloved munchkin.

*9. Thou shalt respect your munchkin cat.*

It's surprising to note that a lot of pet owners bring home a loving and lively pet like a munchkin only to ignore its quirks and munchkin cat personality and treat it like a piece of furniture. Do not be one of those pet owners.

A munchkin kitten or cat is a very social cat breed. Respect its needs and its nature by giving it a little attention when you're home. These interactions can help your munchkin and yourself as well.

### 10. Thou shalt not more abandon your munchkin cat.

Probably the most important rule in these 10 commandments, it is also the saddest and unfortunately the most apt. A lot of new pet owners will bring home a munchkin cat only to discover that having one entails more attention and responsibilities than they are willing to give. This is how our tiny, stubby-legged cat friends end up in shelters more often than not.

Please take the time to read through the chapters on what it means to be a munchkin parent – including the financial demands, the emotional commitment, and the pros and cons – and make an educated and informed decision.

Here's a tip from an experienced cat parent – avoid feline love at first sight! Just like with people, love at first sight, may not work out for the best just because it was emotion-driven and it wasn't an adult, committed decision. Spare yourself and your munchkin the heartbreak and be the prepared pet owner that you need to be.

# Chapter 3 – Where Can I Get a Munchkin Cat?

* * *

You have two choices when you're looking to bring home a munchkin cat - you can adopt from a pet shelter, or you can choose from a cat breeder's munchkin kittens. Both options have its pros and cons, and I couldn't really tell you which one would be better. It all depends on your personal preferences. What I can do is walk you through what cat adoption will be like and what to look for when you're in search of a reputable munchkin cat breeder.

## Munchkin Cat Adoption from a Shelter

There is a lot of good in adopting a pet, especially a munchkin cat. Munchkin cats are friendly, sociable beings and yearn for a family that they can play with and interact with. They won't easily adapt to the limited movement and interaction in a pet shelter and would definitely thrive more in a family setting.

*Figure 9: Don't look past shelters for their potential to provide you with a very loyal Munchkin Cat.*

Thanks to the popularity of cats, there are usually plenty of cat shelters in any given area of the United States. You can start by searching for their information on Google and even specify your search for munchkin cats. Give them a call or look up their information and set up a visit so that you can meet the people working at the shelter as well as the different munchkin kittens or cats that are living there.

Having your heart set on a munchkin cat won't be a problem - rescue shelters have plenty of pure breeds; as much as 25% in fact. Purebred cats like munchkins are abandoned or left behind just as much as mixed breeds. There are even cat rescue groups that offer shelter to specific cat breeds which means that there are cat shelters which specifically look for new homes for abandoned munchkins or dwarf cats. Not only will you be able to give an abandoned munchkin cat a new home, but you also won't have to pay the premium munchkin cat price for your munchkin kitty.

Shelters will usually charge you an adoption fee which means that you will still need to have an adoption budget prepared (which should also cover home preparation for your cat). This fee usually goes to supporting the overhead cost of the shelter as well as funding pet rescues which will be money well spent. The fee should still be a lot less than what you would pay a breeder for a purebred munchkin cat. A typical adoption fee would start at £80 in the UK, $120 in the USA but some shelters would pass on the cost of housing and feeding which would raise the munchkin cat price to about £200 or about $300 in the USA.

Most shelters also offer additional services like spaying or neutering your munchkin kitty, as well as vaccinations, microchipping, and even some toys if you want them. I would advise that you take them up on the spaying or neutering as well as vaccinations, but if you already have a vet in mind to take care of those details for you, then that's perfectly fine. On that note, taking your new munchkin cat to the vet should be your first priority, especially if you have other pets at home.

Pro Tip!

Ask the shelter what they are feeding your munchkin cat so that

you can have the food
preparations done ahead of time.

If you're still feeling unsure of yourself as a cat parent, then take the time to visit a potential cat shelter one of these weekends. Cat rescuers are the best people to talk to about bringing a munchkin cat home and taking care of them. They care just as much as you do when it comes to finding a good and loving home for their cats and will be able to give you a ton of useful information and put your mind at ease.

### Finding a Reputable Munchkin Cat Breeder

There are upsides to getting your munchkin cat from a breeder instead of adopting a cat from a shelter. To start with, adopting a cat means that they have already had a family before you. This could mean that they may already have set behavioral standards and may even need an attitude adjustment. While troubled munchkin cats in shelters deserve a kind and loving home just like anyone else, they may not be the best fit for a first-time cat owner or an inexperienced one. To put it simply, a teenage munchkin cat or even a senior munchkin kitty who has been around the block may be too much for a beginner cat parent to handle. In that case, finding a reputable munchkin cat breeder for munchkin kittens may be your best option. But how do you spot good cat breeders from the bad ones?

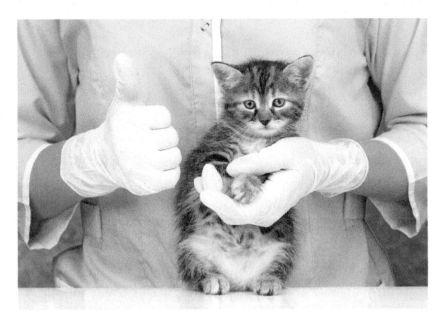

*Figure 10: Breeders should provide full health records, if not look elsewhere!*

A lot of people would ask about awards, certifications, titles, and how long a breeder has been working, but here are some of the warning signs I have learned to look for when visiting a cat breeder:

**1. Has too many breeds, or too many munchkin cats, making the spaces too crowded. (Usually with too few workers.)**

A good munchkin cat breeder will take good care of his or her cats which means giving them enough space to move around in. Having them live in spaces that are too limiting speaks volumes about the breeder. It means that he or she is more concerned about breeding as many munchkin kittens as possible so that more can be sold to make a higher profit, even if it means neglecting their basic needs.

Just because they are dwarf cats or midget cats as some would call them doesn't mean that they don't need just as much space as a regular sized cat.

**2. They talk more about titles; doesn't have a lot to say about the individual munchkin kittens' characteristics.**

When the munchkin cat breeder doesn't have much to say about the munchkin kittens' personalities or character, it means that he or she spends next to zero amount of time with them. This is a neon warning sign for you to go look for a munchkin cat somewhere else. A cat breeder that doesn't spend time with the actual cats is just in it for the profit and doesn't care whether the munchkin cats are taken care of or are up to standard registration.

**3. Only has bad things to say about other munchkin cat breeders.**

What's a sure sign of a good cat breeder? His or her willingness to recommend other cat breeders that they know. For example, if you happen to visit a cat breeder that doesn't have munchkin kittens; the breeder should be able to recommend you to a reputable munchkin cat breeder or another breeder who could give you a recommendation. Cat lovers and those who breed them usually run in the same, tight circles.

**4. Unconcerned about what kind of home you will be providing for the munchkin kittens.**

If they don't care about how well you can take care of the munchkin kittens, then they just don't care about the munchkin cats.

*5. Charges prices that are much too high for things like the size of the munchkin kittens' body or their color or the color patterns.*

The munchkin cat price is about £300 to £600 in the UK and about $300 to $500 in the US on average, but of course, can vary depending on the area you live. This also varies with the food that has been provided, possibly the lineage of the munchkin kittens and the quality of the breeding stock, or the reputation of the breeder. If your breeder is trying to charge you more than that market price based on inconsequential things like supposed rare color patterns or the size of the dwarf cat, they are just trying to make an extra buck at your expense.

There are standard registration size and weight specified for munchkin cats and other dwarf cats or midget cats. The size should not be the basis of a price increase.

Pro Tip!

The market munchkin cat price as of 2016 in the UK is at £300 to £600.

**How to Spot Munchkin Kitten Farms or Kitten Mills**

One source of munchkin cats or munchkin kittens or any other dwarf cats at all costs is a kitten farm or kitten mill.

These places churn out cats like a production line would churn out cars or radios with very little attention given to the well-being of our feline friends. Cat lovers and all pet lovers, in general, do not support these farms because they have very low regard for cats and pets, whether they are munchkin cats, cats of other breeds, or puppies. They tend to be abusive and downright dangerous for munchkins and other pets.

A lot of people, even those who are already cat parents, are surprised to know that most pet stores in the country probably source their pets from mills. A telltale sign is when they insist that they deliver your pet to your doorstep instead of having you come over, meet the munchkin, and see the rest of the munchkin kittens. If they won't let you see the environment, your pet grew up in, and how it was cared for, you are buying from a kitten mill.

Here is how to spot these kitten farms or mills.

1. Sells several different cat breeds. There will be plenty of each kind.
2. Will claim Grand Champions in their breeding stock but will have very little to back the claim up.
3. Breeds for the sole purpose of selling pets. Will have no interest in making the munchkin cat breed or any other breeding line better.
4. May try to charge by the color or appearance of the munchkin cat and not by genetic quality.
5. The munchkin kittens and other pets sold by the breeder will generally look less healthy than those by a reputable breeder.

6. Will insist that they deliver your munchkin cat instead of having you over to visit or choose among the litter.

Please avoid munchkin kitten farms or any other pet farms at all cost for the sake of our pet friends and family. Backyard breeders share a lot of the giveaway traits mentioned above but operate on a much smaller scale. They are no better and would sell you any pet of any genetic quality to make a profit.

**Papers and Documents for Your Munchkin Cat**

When bringing home a munchkin cat or munchkin kitten from an adoption shelter or a breeder, you should be provided with a set of documents that will give you and your vet vital information about your cat.

You will need the following documents:

Vaccine Record
Pedigree

Optional documentation includes:

Health Guarantee or Veterinary Certificate
Microchip Registration

These additional registration forms are optional, depending on your agreement with the breeder or shelter. A microchip registration form will come with the actual microchipping of your munchkin cat if you opt to have it microchipped for added security. In a nutshell, microchipping involves placing a microchip in your pet that will help you track it down if it wanders away. Neutered and spayed cats are less likely to wander away, but it can still prove very useful in the case of cat theft, especially with rare cat breeds.

A vaccine record is, of course, mandatory as is the vaccination of your munchkin cat. For the veterinary certificate or the health certificate, it will only be needed if you are bringing your pet in from a country outside the EU and for traveling within the EU. Basically, you will need the veterinary certificate to apply for an EU pet passport which guarantees that your munchkin cat has received all the necessary vaccination shots at the correct time.

In most cases, your vet should be able to issue a pet passport himself or herself. If not, you can ask them for a referral or contact the Animal and Plant Health Agency.

Some munchkins that have been abandoned and rescued will not have a pedigree that shows their lineage, but there are a lot of munchkin cats in shelters that come with a pedigree. These will be the cats that have been brought to shelters by previous owners for various reasons and came with complete papers and documentation.

*Figure 11: Potential Prey Spotted!*

Pro Tip!

The munchkin cat breed is a relatively new breed. As of now, there are no show quality munchkin pedigrees; only those showing good health.

# Chapter 4 – Understanding a Munchkin Cat's Personality and Temperament

* * *

You've read up on the dwarf cats history; you know the difference between a munchkin cat and a teacup cat, and you know how to spot a bad cat breeder from a mile away. Are you ready to welcome a munchkin cat or even munchkin kittens to your family and home?

Before anything else, you need to get to know the munchkin cat breed a little better. Forget the background information you have on this midget cat breed for a second and try to get to know these munchkins on a more personal level. What are they like? How sociable are they? How intelligent are munchkin cats? How will they respond to you as a cat parent?

Let's take advantage of this chapter to get to know munchkin kittens and cats as we would our new friends.

*Figure 12: Don't let their appearance fool you –*
*Munchkin Cats can be quite athletic!*

Did You Know?

These short-legged cats don't let
their height stop them from doing
some serious climbing. They are
fast and agile climbers, and they
love to show off their climbing
skills!

## Munchkin Cats are a Very Friendly Breed

One of the reasons that people love munchkins isn't just
because they resemble kittens well into adulthood; they
also don't outgrow their kitten-like personality even when
they're all grown up! This is a lot different from your usual
cat personality with the tendency to be aloof or above us
puny humans. They're not afraid to play, to romp, and to

call your attention if they're looking for some munchkin kitty quality time.

They are more social than most cats. On one hand, they'll be perfectly fine by themselves as most cats are, but on the contrary, they thrive in company; especially when they're the center of attention! They're not picky about whom they hang out with either, resembling doggie personality in this aspect more than cats. They make ideal pets in a multi-pet household and will generally get along well with other members of the family, whether they are cats or dogs. I wouldn't expect a munchkin cat to get along well with birds, though. They are still cats with cat-like instincts, don't forget.

While it isn't the kind of cat that you would describe as placid and unruffled, the munchkin cat is even-tempered and affectionate. More words to describe the munchkin is extrovert, outgoing, confident, and loving. Unlike most cats, it loves being hugged and petted and doesn't mind being held. It won't be afraid to climb up close to you for a cuddle (which will be often, believe me).

If you want a cat that loves everyone, the munchkin cat is your best bet.

*Figure 13: Most Munchkin Cats love a good head rub!*

## Munchkin Cats Are Intelligent

One of the most common questions that I get about munchkin cats is, are they trainable? The answer is yes; they most definitely are.

A lot of people get the impression that munchkin kitties tend to be childlike which isn't untrue. With this observation, they assume that a munchkin cat would have a short attention span and would be difficult to train; now this is far from the truth. Munchkins respond very well and very quickly to training, making them ideal household companions.

You can challenge your munchkin cat's mental prowess by teaching it how to do tricks like how to sit and come at command, gifting it with puzzle toys like a treat maze, and interacting with it regularly. The more you interact with your cat, the more you'll gain a human to pet understanding. On that note, your munchkin cat will learn to identify your moods soon enough - happy, displeased, sad - and will respond to them accordingly. It may even push the boundaries a little, checking to see how staunchly you stand by your house rules. Be a good parent and correct it lovingly.

**Munchkin Cats Are Born Explorers**

Munchkins love to map out every nook and cranny of their homes. This short-legged cat is also surprisingly an accomplished climber, and you'll find it exploring the top of bookshelves just as easily as the underside of your coach. More than being your feline Marco Polo, munchkin cats also like to hoard the little, shiny treasures that they find, earning them the nickname 'magpie.'

If you don't want your shiny jewelry, buttons, or nail clippers to go missing, put them away properly where your munchkin can't get at them. It might take forever to find your cat's hiding spot, and you just might never find those pendants ever again.

**Munchkin Cats Are Well-adjusted and Even-tempered**

The two words that are like magic to a cat parent with a big family - well-adjusted and even-tempered.

A munchkin cat won't be frail and fearful, even for its first night in your house. It takes to new environments well, even welcomes them; especially since it's a chance to explore new territory. Give it a couple of days and your munchkin cat will know your house like it has been there for years.

Munchkins are also one of the most even-tempered cat breeds there is. Even when it is surprised or if it handled a little more roughly than it wants, a munchkin cat's claws don't usually come out. Instead, it will prefer just to leave and go to a more secluded part of the house for some peace and quiet or look for something else to play with.

*Figure 14: Partners in crime? Munchkin Cats get along well with children- socialize early!*

## Munchkin Cats Are Low Maintenance

Most cats are low maintenance and munchkin cats are no

exception. They are well able to clean themselves and will most likely hone in on the litter box in your home to do their business. While they are energetic, they are not hyperactive and moderate play will satisfy its need for exercise.

Even though munchkin cats and munchkin kittens love attention, it is not very demanding and will choose to amuse itself if you're busy. Spending 10 to 15 minutes a day cuddling with your munchkin, playing, and rubbing its belly is enough to keep it happy. It's the perfect cat for inexperienced cat parents.

Pro Tip!

Munchkin cats are not hypoallergenic.

# Chapter 5 – How to Choose the Right Munchkin Cat for You

\* \* \*

You're finally ready to bring a munchkin cat into your home. You've read the books, you've talked to family and friends, and today is the day. You walk through the doors of a pet shelter or the munchkin breeder you picked out, and then you realize a huge problem. How are you ever going to choose just one cat out of the many munchkin kittens or cats that are waiting to be loved and cared for?

Resist the urge to simply bring them all home with you for a second and try to remember that the commitment you are making on that big day will have to last as long as 14 to 15 years. Also, this may sound harsh, but not all munchkin cats or dwarf cats or munchkin kittens will be a good fit for a human family, despite their genetic disposition to be friendly and smart.

There are plenty of things to consider when you're planning to bring a munchkin cat home to become part of your family. These things include health, disposition, age, and even appearance. We'll walk you through how to find the munchkin cat that will be an excellent fit for you and your family.

## What is the Ideal Pet Munchkin Cat?

Not all munchkin cats are the same in the same way that not all dogs of the same breed are the same. Some munchkins that you'll meet will be more aggressive that their families can't possibly have other pets in the house. Others are so meek that only the humans they live with can pet them. Others are afraid of being handled by anyone while some may want to horde the attention of the entire household.

Your munchkin cat's disposition and personality are molded by a lot of different factors. In terms of genetics, munchkin cats and munchkin kittens are predisposed to being friendly, moderately active, affectionate, intelligent, and fun-loving; but it's not only about the genes. The other factors are decided by the munchkin's environment, the classic case of nurture vs. nature.

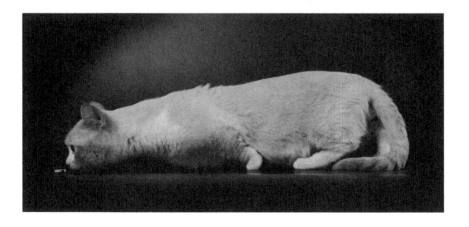

*Figure 15: On the prowl again!*

Cats that you'll find on the street are naturally more feral because they have to struggle to survive and to feed. They were not born feral or aggressive or unsociable; it just learned those traits from its environment and from the other cats who come out on top in the same social circle.

An ideal household pet, on the other hand, would not make a show of aggressiveness. It would be sociable and friendly around other people, especially with kids. They understand the rules and won't throw a tantrum when they don't get what they want. Think of a well-raised, well-mannered child; the well-mannered munchkin cat would not be so different.

The problem is, a lot of a munchkin cat's disposition is already decided by the time that you meet it. That's why this chapter on how to choose the right munchkin cat for your family is so important so that you can learn the tell-tale signs of behavioral problems and bring home a well-adjusted, socialized munchkin cat.

## Hand-reared or Orphan Cats vs. Litter Munchkin Kittens

The truth is, hand-reared cats or orphan cats are at a much higher risk of displaying behavioral problems than those who grew up with their own mothers and with other munchkin kittens. When they're with their mother growing and are part of a litter, munchkin kittens will have a clear and immediate authority figure in the form of the mother munchkin cat. They're subjected to more frustration like having to wait until their mother lets them feed and having to tussle a little with the other munchkin kittens before they can do so. This way, they also learn how to cope with frustration, and they learn to be patient and not throw a fit when they don't get what they want.

By simply learning how to live with other munchkin kittens who may want to play when they don't or who wake them when they want to sleep, they learn a few guidelines with how to live and play well with others. At a young age, they know that biting, scratching, and other forms of aggressiveness are unwelcome (and will not be tolerated by the mother munchkin).

Pro Tip!

Munchkin kittens should at least be 9 weeks of age before you can bring it home. For pedigree kittens, breeders will usually wait until they are 12 weeks old.

You will most likely find hand-reared cats or orphan cats in shelters because cat breeders usually let munchkin kittens stay with the mother cat to feed and to socialize with other kittens until a certain age.

I'm not saying that you should write them off completely. Just keep in mind that these cats will need a more experienced hand in raising and loving them and will not be a good fit for beginner cat parents. Some hand-reared or orphan cats with behavioral problems would have already been trained and appropriately socialized by cat rescuers and shelters and will still make excellent household pets.

Good pet shelters will not keep pets locked up the entire day. Most will interact with the pets and try to expose them to the normal environment of a human home, like the noise of a TV, the sounds people make when they're doing their daily routines like cooking or talking or watching a football game. This way, pets can adjust to the new normal and won't be as frightened when they are adopted.

Also, this is not to say that humans should not be part of the equation during the earliest stages of kitten growth. Rather, it's the opposite. If kittens don't meet their first humans early on, then people will never be a part of what they consider 'normal.' It's just as important for munchkin kittens to be exposed to gentle handling from humans, but all within the limited social circle of its litter.

## What is the Right Age to Bring a Munchkin Cat Home?

The rule of thumb in bringing a munchkin kitten home is that it should be at least 9 weeks old, two weeks older than when it would be appropriate to bring home a puppy. To be safe, some breeders would even recommend not to bring munchkin kittens home until they are 12 weeks of age. That's because kittens need to spend a lot of the early stage of their life with their mother and other kittens of the litter. Being with their munchkin cat family is the best way that they can learn how to socialize with others and how not to be too aggressive but also how not to be too meek or withdrawn.

## Should You Choose an Adult or Kitten Munchkin Cat?

There are pros and cons in bringing home either a grown up munchkin cat or a baby kitten, and it all comes down to how much you are prepared to handle.

Of course, most people would think of a munchkin kitten when they're considering bringing home a munchkin to their home and why shouldn't they? Kittens are very cute and fluffy and playful! It's hard to deny the appeal of those large eyes, the endless curiosity, and their seemingly innate attachment to their new family. Having a kitten, especially a munchkin kitten, in your home can be plenty of fun!

On the other hand, raising a munchkin kitten can be a ton of work! Kittens are easily distracted (in the same way that children are easily distracted), and munchkin kittens are even worse when it comes to this particular trait. Their intelligence gives them almost endless curiosity and it will be hard to get their attention. For those first few days of training them and teaching them the house rules, you will need endless amounts of patience.

Also because of the same curiosity, you might end up in the veterinary clinic a lot more times than you would expect if you bring home a munchkin kitten instead of a cat. A lot of cat lovers swear that most of a cat's nine lives will be used for these early stages of development because they are endlessly exploring and trying new things. Be prepared to pick up your munchkin kitten from under the couch, on the drapes, or even stuck between the fridge and the kitchen counter.

Consider the natural inquisitiveness of a regular kitten and imagine how a munchkin kitten can be like with its already innate explorer personality. Which reminds me, you will definitely need to look into kitten proofing your house, another added expense.

The pro side of bringing home a munchkin kitten instead of a grown cat is that you will have a playful, tumbling, ball of energy baby munchkin in your home. It will be a source of endless joy and affection, and you will have a lot of fun! Just keep your impatience in check and remember that you are dealing with a baby in your midst.

Munchkin kittens would not be the best choice for families with very young children because you will be running yourself ragged trying to take care of all the babies in the house. On the other hand, they will make for a great fit with older, more responsible kids.

In terms of munchkin cat price, kittens are often more expensive than adult munchkin cats.

An adult munchkin cat will also have its own pros and cons. One of the biggest cons for most cat lovers, especially new cat parents, are that they just aren't as goofy or as playful or as cute as munchkin kittens! Kittens definitely have the upper hand when it comes to being adorable. But if you don't want to deal with the antics of a much younger cat or if you're worried about your young kids not handling your pets gently enough, then a more mature and stable grown up munchkin cat may be the better option.

Also, while you don't know exactly how your munchkin kitten will grow up in terms of appearance and personality, you already know what you're going to get with a grown up munchkin cat. Its temper won't change unless something drastic happens, it's coat is already the way it's going to be for the rest of its life, and you simply won't get any surprises.

Personally, I feel the best part of bringing home an adult munchkin cat over munchkin kittens is that I won't need to cat proof my home as much. Finding my cat stuck in nooks of the house will also be unlikely and trips to the vet will be less. That's a lot of expenses that I won't have to make.

The biggest argument for bringing home an adult munchkin cat is that most of them have very slim chances of finding a new human family. A lot of these cats are excellent pets in terms of disposition, temperament, health, and appearance and have become orphaned cats because their owners didn't know what they were signing up for or they had to move to another state or simply didn't have the finances to support a pet.

However, a grown up munchkin cat will be at a much higher risk of having behavioral problems, like not knowing how to use a litter box or are too quick to show aggression. Good shelters will disclose all of these issues to possible cat parent candidates so that you know what you're getting into. And while I am a firm believer that all pets can be rehabilitated out of bad behavior, I would not recommend beginner munchkin cat parents to take on this big responsibility.

## Choosing the Munchkin Cat for You

The factors that you want to be keeping an eye out for when you're choosing the munchkin cat for you are appearance, disposition or personality, and health. I will leave choosing the look of the munchkin cat up to you and your personal preferences. Instead, let's talk about how to find cats or kittens with an amiable personality – just the right confidence and sociable outlook – and how to look out for possible health problems.

> Did You Know?
>
> Some cats will have extra toes, a condition called polydactyly. This does not present any coordination issues or health problems.

### 1. Talk to the breeder or the shelter volunteers.

This is the first step that you should take when choosing a munchkin cat. Ask the people in charge whether the cats or kittens were raised together with the mommy cat and the litter. Ask them if the cats are brought out every day so that they can interact with people. Do they play with the cats themselves? Do they feed the cats themselves?

*Figure 16: Teaching children to look after their Munchkin Cat is a good way to help them learn life skills.*

The best way to find a good, well-adjusted munchkin cat is to ask the people in charge for their favorites or their recommendations. You would be surprised at how well they will know the cats and how much of the cats' personalities they're familiar with.

If you have another pet in your house, like a dog, ask if the munchkin cats have had any exposure to other pet animals. It's always better to have a munchkin cat that has already met dogs if you've got one at home in the same way that you want them exposed to people growing up. While munchkin cats are naturally friendly, there is an understandable adjustment period, and you want to make sure that all your babies get along and won't be a danger to each other.

*2. Watch how the munchkin cats or kittens interact with others.*

What you want is a munchkin cat or kitten that is playful but isn't too aggressive. Try to watch how they play and see how well they get along with others. Is the cat showing the signs of a bad temper? Is it playful and interactive? How well does it take being bothered or played with by the other cats or kittens? Is the cat acting like a bully by pushing the other munchkins around?

I would encourage you to choose the cat that plays with others but doesn't insist on winning every wrestling match and takes well to the physical contact with other cats. Avoid those that stick to the corners to prevent any contact or playtime with the other cats because they will probably be too meek for a good pet.

*3. See how the munchkin cat or munchkin kitten responds to you.*

Ask the breeder or the people at the shelter if you can handle the cat. The cat should show confidence in meeting you but should not be overly aggressive and try to show you that it is the boss. It should not cower in fear when you try petting it or try to bite you or pull away.

Try cradling it in your arms to see how well the munchkin cat responds to you. Does it accept your petting naturally? Does it act in a friendly way towards you?

## 4. *Assess the munchkin cat's health.*

It is just as important to bring home a healthy cat as much as a well-adjusted cat. Here are the signs that you should look for to show good health.

- Eyes are clear and free of discharge.
- Nose should be free of discharge.
- Ears should be clean, without any blockage, and without any odor. There should be no black, granular discharge.
- Ears should not be irritated which can be spotted if the munchkin cat is excessively scratching the area.
- Gums should look pink and healthy, without any ulcers or bleeding.
- Coat should be clean and soft to the touch. There should be no signs of lice or fleas. Sign of parasites can include like tiny black or black-red granules, bald spots, or excessive scratching.
- Anal area should be clean, without any matted fur. There should be no signs of parasites; having tapeworm will show in this area as similar to cucumber seeds.
- Belly should not be protruding which can be a sign of parasite infection.
- Head should not be experiencing tremors.

Make sure that you are aware of the quirks of the particular cat breed before making your health assessment. For example, a Scottish fold munchkin will naturally have short-looking, folded ears as part of its genetic disposition.

Pro Tip!

Munchkin kittens' coats will
usually not appear as glossy as an
adult cat's coat.

Knowledge and information are key to having a loving, healthy, and well-socialized pet munchkin. Being prepared is an important part of being a good parent and ignorance should never be an excuse to encourage ill treatment of a munchkin cat or for breeding or bringing home a munchkin cat that is unhealthy and ill-suited to become a pet.

**Ask if the Munchkin Cat Has Insurance**

Cat insurance is more common in the UK than it is in the United States. If your munchkin cat does have insurance, the common practice is that it should last 6 weeks after you bring it home with you. Insurance should also cover health issues and benefits. When the breeder-provided insurance runs out, the insurance company will usually call the new cat parents if they want to continue the insurance for their munchkin cat.

If you plan on getting your munchkin cat insurance, make sure that veterinary fees are covered. It is by far the most important form of insurance for your pet, one that you will most likely need during its first year growing up.

Munchkin kittens get into all kinds of trouble, and you will find yourself helping them out if different fixes on a daily basis.

Before you decide to keep the insurance or get your munchkin cat insured, be sure to check what the policy actually covers.

The cost of cat insurance in the UK will depend on the coverage you choose, the kind of pet you have, and whether it is microchipped. Having a microchipped pet will reduce the cost of the insurance. A standard plan which usually covers 'accidents only' will usually cost about £35 to £50 while a lifetime coverage can cost you £50 to £200, depending on the insurance provider.

**Be Prepared to Walk Away**

You've come this far, and your heart is set on having a munchkin cat or munchkin kitten when you get home. The problem is, you can't seem to find one that is a good fit for you or your family. Here's the part where you have to steel yourself and walk away.

Walking away from having your own munchkin cat while you're standing in the middle of cute, adorable munchkin cats or kittens can be very tough (some would say impossible), but it's the right thing to do if you don't feel 100% about the cat you will be bringing home.

Remember, you are making a commitment that should last for more than a decade. For your munchkin cat, it is a lifetime commitment. You need to be absolutely sure before you choose a munchkin cat and call it part of the family. If the cat is showing health problems or is too aggressive or too meek, do not bring it home with you even if it has the most beautiful coat you've ever seen on a cat or the most adorable eyes. The saddest story of any pet is when it is abandoned by its family because it turned out that it was too much to handle. This is true for munchkin cats as for any pet; you'll find dozens of munchkins in shelters all over the US.

## Visit the Munchkin Cats Ahead of Time

To avoid any heartache, the first time you see the munchkin cats should not be the day you plan to bring them home. Good cat breeders will usually let you meet the cats and even handle them long before they are ready to be brought home. That way, you can get to know the kittens in the litter and get to know them early on.

It would be ideal if you could visit different cat breeders so that you can meet different munchkin cats (and get different munchkin cat price options too) but try not to go from breeder to breeder petting different cats. You may be carrying a virus that could hurt more vulnerable cats, especially the young ones. If your breeder politely asks you to refrain from petting the cats, this is probably the reason. Remember always to ask permission before touching the cats.

A good breeder will always check if you are capable of caring for the munchkin cats. They may have just as many questions for you as you do for them. The same goes for cat rescuers who work at the shelters. Their interest in you and your ability to care for your pet munchkin is a good sign to look out for. It means that they are taking good care of the cats and are raising them well.

# Chapter 6 – Preparing Your Home for Your New Munchkin Cat

* * *

The big day has finally arrived! You are ready to welcome your new short-legged cat into your home. But here's the big question – is your home ready for your new munchkin cat?

Bringing home a new cat is just like bringing home a baby for the first time. You need to make sure that your home is a healthy, but also safe, place for your new munchkin to live in. And just like with children, you also need to protect your munchkin cat from getting hurt with rough play or just being too inquisitive.

There is an entire section below where we talk about the basic items that you can buy for your munchkin cat but, understandably, the first step to preparing your home is always about cat-proofing.

## How to Cat-Proof Your Home for Your New Munchkin Cat

This part of the chapter is for basic cat-proofing, steps you have to take for your munchkin's safety when you are bringing a munchkin cat home to live with you.

As you may have already guessed, munchkin cats need a

little more house proofing than other cat breeds. It's because of their love for exploring, and they're more active and more playful than other cats. Mixed munchkin breeds like the Scottish fold munchkin or the Persian munchkin might not need as much house proofing as a pure munchkin cat, but I would recommend that you err on the side of caution.

## 1. Remove all poisonous plants inside and outside your house.

This is a given for any home that has pets and children. The last thing that you want inside your house are toxic plants that can poison and very seriously hurt the unwitting. These toxic plants can have adverse effects that range from mild poisoning to making your munchkin cat or munchkin kittens very sick to potentially lethal. But how do you know if your plant is toxic or poisonous?

You would be surprised how some of the most unassuming and common decorative plants are actually toxic for most pets and people. Here's a quick rundown of these "cute killers":

- Poinsettia
- Easter Lily
- Larkspur
- Aloe Vera
- Azalea
- Dumb Cane
- Oleander
- Foxglove

- Angel's Trumpet
- Water Hemlock
- English Yew
- Snakeroot
- Daffodil
- Rhododendron

*Figure 17: It's extremely important to ensure no toxic plants can be reached by your Munchkin Cat.*

These plants listed above are toxic when ingested. I would assume that you have not decorated your home with plants that are toxic to the touch. If you have any doubts, it would be best to ask your local florist.

*2. Keep your cleaning supplies in a storage area for this specific purpose. Make sure that the storage area can be closed up.*

You would be surprised how easily your pets, especially curious munchkin cats, can get to your cleaning supplies. Sealed bottles will be unsealed; plastic containers will be leaked; trust me, I have seen this happen countless times.

*Figure 18: Just as with humans, cleaning supplies and other chemicals can be quite harmful. Keep out of the reach of your Munchkin Cat.*

The best way to keep your munchkin cat or munchkin kittens away from these toxic chemicals is to find a space that can be closed off, like a cabinet under the sink, to keep them stored at all times. You don't have to lock the cabinet or container; you just need to be able to close it so that no curious cat can get to it.

It's also important to make sure that the whole family - kids included - knows where to put the cleaning supplies

and to put them away immediately after they're used. It is never good to leave them lying around the house, especially the kitchen where food is prepared. If you have kids in the house, then you should definitely invest in a lock.

On the list of possible poisonous household items to cats, are potpourri and toilet bowl cleaners left in the toilet water.

*3. Make sure that all medication is kept in a special medicine kit or cabinet, safely out of reach.*

Some medicine for humans is deadly to cats in even the smallest doses. Keep your munchkin cat safe by not leaving your medication lying around, whether they are in sealable bottles or in those foil packets. To be on the safe side, always keep all of the medicine in the house in a special medicine kit or cabinet. This way, it will be out of reach to any munchkin cats and pets, plus your family will always know where to get medical supplies in case of an accident.

**4. Unplug appliances that aren't in use or tuck them away, out of reach.**

*Figure 19: Electrical cords can present both a choking as well as an electric shock hazard to your Munchkin Cat. Conceal them where possible.*

Plugged appliances and electrical cords pose as one of the biggest hazards to munchkin cats in any household, especially munchkin kittens. The short legs make it even worse. Imagine your munchkin baby chewing on a plugged, electrical cord. More than just getting a shock, it could prove to be a lethal experience for your pet.

It's important to take precautions by unplugging your appliances when they are not in use. Don't leave the electrical cords just lying around the floor exposed either.

As a matter of fact now might be a good time to invest in some wire guards. They keep the wires away from your munchkins while also keeping your home neater.

If you use power supply strips, then it's crucial to cover it up with an outlet cover which is sold for child safety but will do just as well to keep your munchkin baby safe. If you don't absolutely have to use a power supply strip, then don't. These things are hazardous and using one all the time in your home will not end well for your munchkin cat.

### 5. Cords and draperies should be coiled or tied neatly up in a knot.

Aside from electrocuting your munchkin cat, cords as well as draperies should be tied up or neatly bundled up so that your munchkin cat won't get entangled in the mess. Or worse, accidentally strangle itself. For draperies, tie them up into neat knots. For cords and cables, you can use a cable winder to tuck them away.

### 6. Always keep the dryer closed and always check it before closing.

One of the horror stories that every cat parent is afraid of is forgetting to check the dryer and accidentally leaving their pet in there, subject to hunger, thirst, and even suffocation. Let's not even get started on what-ifs, like what if someone turns the dryer on with your munchkin cat still in there. Save yourself the worry and paranoia and make a habit of checking the dryer for your munchkin cat every time you close it.

If you're wondering how high the risk is of your munchkin cat climbing its way in there, the chances are actually very high. Munchkins love these small and warm spaces, not too different from a cat crate. They take to it like they would a cat cave, a special little nook just for them. Your worries are warranted which is why you have to be vigilant about this. It's also important to explain to other family members that you're not just paranoid and that they should always check the dryer before closing it too.

*7. Install switch covers for your disposal switch. Make sure it is closed unless you plan to use it.*

We love our munchkin cats because they are cute and small, but it also means that they are in a bigger danger with the disposal unit than other regular cats. In case you're wondering, dwarf cats and midget cats have had trouble with disposal units before, though thankfully not all end with the loss of a pet. To make sure your munchkin cat is safe, installing a switch cover over the disposal switch should be on the top of your list.

*8. Make sure your garbage is stored in a lidded container that shuts to keep your munchkin cat out.*

This will save you a lot of trouble and your munchkin cat from any danger of choking or poisoning. If you have a munchkin cat or any pet in your home, it is important to have a lidded trash bin to keep them from 'exploring' the garbage. You won't have to wake up to last night's trash all over the kitchen floor or to a very sick munchkin cat.

## 9. Check for small choking hazards.

On the topic of choking and choking hazards, it is also important to make sure that any small objects like a child's toys should be placed in special containers designated for just that purpose. A munchkin cat is something of a hoarder, and it will find small objects like a plastic army soldier interesting. Prevent the possibility of choking by making sure that these objects are out of reach for your munchkin.

## 10. Put away any shiny trinkets like jewelry.

This is a precaution that is specifically meant for the munchkin cat. The munchkin cat isn't called the magpie without reason. It takes to shiny pretties like a pirate and will not only admire your jewelry it will also put it away in its special hiding place. Believe me when I say that these hiding places are impossible to find, given this little midget cat's size. Avoid getting a headache and just put your valuables away in a safe box where your adorable little munchkin cat can't find them.

## 11. Make sure your shelves are secure.

One of the first things that a munchkin cat will do in a new environment is explore, explore, explore. If you don't want your shelves and books to come crashing down because of the added weight, you need to make sure that they are secure and that they are screwed on tight to your wall or to something that is stable. While we're on the topic, it also wouldn't hurt to secure your curtains as best as you can.

## 12. Secure the screens.

Munchkin cats just love to climb! You'll soon find out that they'll climb anything, including your window screens. To prevent the screens from collapsing because of the added weight, make sure that they are secure to avoid any damage or any injuries.

## 13. Keep the toilet bowl closed.

Munchkin cats are especially prone to falling into the toilet bowl while trying to drink from it because of their size. This is particularly dangerous when you use a treatment chemical for keeping your toilet bowl water clean and disinfected because the liquid is basically poison. And there's also the risk of drowning.

Just to be on the safe side, always make sure that your toilet bowl is closed when it isn't in use.

## Building a Home for Your Munchkin Cat

*Figure 20: It doesn't need to be this perfect; just ensure that your Munchkin Cat's bed is warm, secure, and comfortable.*

Now that you're absolutely sure that your home is safe for your munchkin cat, it's time to take the most fun step of building a home for your new pet. That is, creating spaces for your munchkin that is just his or hers. I like to call these spaces the cat base camp, particularly essential for the first night that your munchkin cat is with you.

It's important to remember that routine is important for a munchkin cat, just like any other cat but if its new territory is too large, it can be pretty overwhelming. That's why setting up a base camp for your new cat is important, giving your new pet a "home base".

The first step is to choose where you're going to place your munchkin's base camp. A bathroom is an ideal size but the water running through pipes or people coming at night could spook your new pet. Your living room can work, but you'll need to cover up all the hiding places which could mean stuffing comforters under the couch. A spare bedroom will also work just as well; you can move your munchkin somewhere else when it has already adjusted to its new environment.

Here are the basics that you're going to need to greet your new munchkin cat or munchkin kitten with:

### 1. Litter box

If you have nothing else, have a litter box. Cats are different from dogs in the sense that they require very little housebreaking. This applies particularly to the munchkin cat because of its innate intelligence. All you need to do is place the litter box in the designated base camp (you can move it somewhere else after the first couple of nights), and your munchkin cat will know to do its business inside the box.

A good rule to follow when it comes to your cat's litter box is to keep it simple, even when choosing and buying one. As a cat parent, I have never bought those high-tech litter boxes that do everything short of cleaning itself out, so I don't know just how much convenience it offers. I find that a simple litter box that's the right size, rectangular in shape, and the correct depth works just fine.

If you buy a litter box that's too small, you can be sure that your munchkin cat will find a different place to soil in next to no time. Buy a litter box that is big enough for your cat to get its business done a few times without having to step on already soiled areas. The litter will need to be scooped twice a day. The box will need to be cleaned more if you're using unscoopable litter.

Aside from size, the other important factor to consider is location. The location of the litter box needs to be convenient and accessible for your munchkin cat. I don't blame you for wanting to place the litter box as far away from your living areas as possible, but if you need a GPS to find it, your cat will probably never use it. Also, the litter box shouldn't be near your munchkin's dishes because no one wants to do their business right beside where they eat.

Here's the piece of cat parenting advice that no one wants to hear - you need one litter box for every cat.

## 2. Dishes

You will need two dishes for your munchkin cat - one for food and one for water.

I would highly recommend that you avoid plastic dishes because most cats are allergic to plastic and develop a skin condition that looks a lot like acne. Also, plastic tends to nick and scratch in small ways that are difficult to notice but ultimately lead to wounded gums and skin. Most veterinarians recommend stainless steel dishes or ceramic dishes (that aren't finished with lead).

It's also a good idea to invest in feeding mats that anchor the dishes to keep them from moving around and avoiding spills. Don't forget to keep the dishes clean to avoid bacterial growth that could cause sickness.

Choosing between dishes and bowls? Dishes are the clear winner because it offers a flat surface. Munchkin cats, like any cats, use their whiskers to navigate, which means they are sensitive and serve a greater purpose than for looks. A bowl with sides, especially tall, straight sides, will irritate the whiskers as they touch while your cat is eating. If you're using a feeding bowl instead of a dish and notice that the feeding area is always messy or that the food is often left uneaten, the brand or flavor of the food may not be the problem.

### 3. Scratching post

The scratching post is for your benefit as much as your munchkin cat and especially for your munchkin kitten. The main purpose of the scratching post is to give your munchkin something to scratch other than your doors or furniture, saving your house from damage and from having scratches on all surfaces.

When buying a scratching post, choose one that is tall enough for your munchkin cat to stretch out on. Some good choices for scratching post material is wood, carpet, sisal rope, and even corrugated cardboard. Make sure that it is sturdy enough to stand even with your cat leaning on it and scratching it.

Scratching posts are best placed beside your munchkin cat's sleeping area or bed, close to where it likes to sleep. You can train your munchkin to use the post by redirecting it when you see it scratching other things like furniture. Just transfer them to the post and help it with the motions of scratching. You can also get a good scratching routine started by gently helping it with scratching motions in the morning and during the evening. You can reward your munchkin when it uses the scratching post with a treat.

You can make sure your home stays scratch free by confining your munchkin cat within a certain space. Once your munchkin is used to the post and scratches it regularly, you can allow it into the rest of the house. In housebreaking your munchkin cat, discipline is key. Help it understand that some things are a privilege, not a right.

**Your Munchkin Cat's First Night**

The first night that your munchkin cat or munchkin kitten spends in your new home is crucial. You want to make a good first impression and create a strong and lasting relationship.

When you bring your munchkin cat home, it will probably be in a carrier. The base camp for your cat should already be ready, with a scratching post, dishes for food and water, and a litter box that's further away from the rest. It's a good idea to have a wet meal waiting the first time your munchkin sees the base camp. The base camp should be in an area that can be closed off or confined. Before releasing your new baby munchkin, make sure that the room is closed. There should be only one other person in the room when you first let your munchkin out of the carrier. It would be better if it's just you and your new baby munchkin.

Set the carrier near the scratching post and open it. Just leave it open and let your munchkin take its time; it will exit the carrier when it is ready. Speak very gently and encouragingly, in low tones. If it comes towards you, gently pet it. If it tries to hide, give it time to leave on its own. It's crucial that the first night should be positive and gently and unchallenging for your munchkin.

That doesn't mean you can't keep your new baby company. Sit with it when it eats the wet meal. After an hour, it should be more open to meeting other people. Make sure that they meet the new munchkin one at a time. Avoid overwhelming your new pet.

With munchkins the way they naturally are, it won't be as shy as most cats. You'll have a playful, fun loving fur ball in next to no time.

## Chapter 7 – Feeding Your New Munchkin Cat

\* \* \*

The difference between and cats – including midget cats – is that they are carnivores, and that's an important difference to understand. Our munchkin cats can't eat like us, and we can't eat like them. This difference also means that they can't eat like dogs who, like us, are omnivores. A dog can stay healthy with a varied diet, eating different kinds of food. Cats, on the other hand, can only eat a narrow range of food to stay healthy.

*Figure 21: Ever eager if tempted by treats, just be sure not to over-feed your Munchkin Cat!*

But then there's cat food, right? Made especially for cats which means that all you need to do is buy cat food, and you've done right by your munchkin cat. There's one problem, though; there are hundreds of cat food brands out there. A quick stroll down the cat food aisle in the grocery store will tell you how true this is. Also, there's the question of how often should you feed your munchkin cat?

These questions, along with a few more, will be answered in this chapter, right down to the nutritional needs of your munchkin cat and the most common mistakes that cat parents make when it comes to feeding.

## What is the Best Diet for Your Munchkin Cat?

Munchkin cats thrive on a high protein diet. The most nutritious meal that you can give your munchkin is a low carbohydrate, high protein meal that consists more of animal protein than plant protein. As carnivores, cats simply do not digest carbohydrates well.

## Is Wet Food or Dry Food Better for Your Munchkin Cat?

Whether or not wet food or dry food is better for your cat is an ongoing heated debate among cat parents. Munchkins cats aren't fussy eaters, so the only question here is which kind of cat food is more nutritious or healthy for your munchkin baby than the other.

Personally, I use wet food for my cats. My qualms with dry food are that they often contain too many carbohydrates that cats, in general, have a hard time digesting, and usually use a lot more plant protein than animal protein as its ingredient. And then there's the low water content. Dry cat food also tends to be highly processed and has very little nutritional value; not something you want for your munchkin baby.

That being said, a lot of my friends' cats have been on dry food and their veterinarian says they are shining examples of feline health. If you do want to feed your munchkin cat dry food, make sure that it gets more water throughout the day to stay well hydrated.

Want to mix the wet and dry food? Not a problem, a lot of cats actually take to the mix a lot better than if they were only fed wet food or dry food.

## How Often Should You Feed Your Munchkin Cat?

The important thing to remember when you're considering how often to feed your munchkin cat is that age is very important. Munchkin cats in different stages of life will have different dietary needs.

Munchkin kittens will typically require more food per pound of body weight which means that they will need to be fed two or three times a day. Because of their size, munchkin kittens don't need as much food as a regular sized kitten. When your munchkin cat is six months to a year old, you can reduce how often you feed it to twice a day, once in the morning and once in the afternoon or early evening. When your munchkin cat is a fully grown adult, which occurs at about one-year-old, once a day feeding will be fine.

The amount of food that you give your cat will depend on several factors. These factors are the quality of the food, the size of the cat, how energetic versus how placid your cat is, and whether you are feeding them dry food versus wet food. If you are feeding your cat high-quality food, they won't have to eat as much of it to meet their dietary needs. You will also need to feed your cat a little bit more food when they tend towards the most active side of the spectrum. Also, it's important to remember that your munchkin cat will need more water when you are feeding it dry food.

Munchkin cats have an active rating that is considered medium by most veterinarians - not too placid, not overactive. For munchkin kittens, 1/3 cup of food two or three times a day is a good rule of thumb to follow. Munchkin cats that are between six months to a year old will do well with half a cup to 3/4 of a cup twice a day. An adult munchkin cat can be fed once a day with half a cup to 3/4 of a cup.

**How to Choose the Right Cat Food For Your Munchkin Cat**

What makes a good cat food stand out from the rest? Forget the labels that say premium or gourmet or organic. The important thing to check when you're buying cat food is the nutritional content. The best way to go is just to ignore whatever marketing lingo they've got going on in front. Go straight to the back where the ingredients are listed to see precisely what you're feeding your munchkin cat.

*Figure 22: As mentioned, look for high protein ingredients near the top of the list for cat food.*

The ingredient that has the highest percentage content in the food should be listed first too, with the least used ingredients down at the bottom. If you are buying 'Chicken Cat Food' for example, chicken should be on top of the ingredients list. It should also make up 95% of the cat food, as required by regulations. Along with the main source of protein, Taurine and water along with vitamins, minerals, enzymes and fatty acids should also be listed at the top.

While preservatives are necessary to keep the food as fresh as possible, a lot of cat food brands add fillers to make it seem like there's more. These fillers such as corn, wheat, rice, or binders can be acceptable at low levels but becomes unacceptable when there's too much of it. Better quality brands will always have less artificial flavors and fillers.

Some of the ingredients to avoid when choosing a cat food

brand for your munchkin cat include the following.

- Byproducts, meat or bone meal
- Cornmeal
- Too many carb fillers
- BHA, BHT, ethoxyquin, and propyl gallate

**The Common Mistakes Cat Parents Make When Feeding Munchkin Cats**

As cat parents, we all make mistakes now and then, but when it comes to feeding our beloved munchkin cats or munchkin kittens, it's always best to be extra careful. Here are the most common mistakes that cat parents make when it comes to feeding cats, even midget cats.

*Figure 23: This might just be a slightly too large serving for this little fellow!*

## 1. Feeding the munchkin cat too much.

There is a general rise in munchkin cat obesity all over the country and it is directly caused by well-meaning cat parents who are afraid they aren't feeding their cats enough. Or they simply can't say no to those adorable munchkin eyes when the little one wants another treat.

Feeding your munchkin cat too much can lead to health complications like diabetes which can shorten the lifespan of your adorable pet. Don't give in to your cat's cravings and save yourself the heartache from making them go on a diet when they get too fat or losing them to diabetes.

## 2. Giving the munchkin cat food that has too many carbohydrates.

This is very common among cat parents who feel that our munchkin cats can eat the same things that we do. Cats do not thrive on rice or wheat or bread. They are natural hunters, and they can easily live on raw meat. They need a diet mostly made up of animal protein that a good cat food brand can provide.

## 3. Feeding munchkin cats food that is bad for cats.

Picture this. You're eating a snack while watching a TV show then your adorable midget cat snuggles up beside you and adorably eyes the food. It feels like the most natural thing to do is offer a treat to your munchkin. The problem is, you don't know whether you are about to feed your munchkin cat or kitten poison. Don't forget, the food that's okay for people may be toxic for cats.

Here are some of the common food that munchkin cats can't eat.

- Onions, garlic, chives
- Milk and other dairy products
- Alcohol
- Grapes, raisins
- Caffeine
- Chocolate!
- Candy
- Fat trimmings, bones
- Raw eggs
- Dog food
- Yeast dough

**4. Feeding the munchkin cat only dry food or not offering enough water.**

Munchkin cats, like most cats, don't drink water as often as they should, unlike dogs who always willingly drink water. They're just more used to getting a lot of the moisture that they need from the food that they eat. The low water intake makes them at risk for health problems like urinary tract infection. You can solve this problem by feeding them wet food or occasionally switching to wet food over dry food or a mix of both.

You can also encourage them to drink more water by always having some available for them. Some cats can detect the slight chlorine in tap water and may refuse to drink it. Try to see if your munchkin cat responds better to bottled water.

## 5. Unknowingly encouraging nutritional deficiencies.

There is a growing trend among munchkin cat parents where they cook or make their own cat food. It's supposed to be more organic in the same way that cooking our own food and avoiding processed food is healthier for people. The problem with this is the usual nutritional needs that cats have are often overlooked. For example, a cat – munchkin cats included – will usually also eat the bone of its prey for more calcium. In most cases, homemade cat food will fail to include this dietary need.

## 6. Cat Treats and Your Munchkin Cat

Cat treats come in handy, especially when you're training your munchkin cat or when you're just trying to win it over. It doesn't hurt to indulge your cute munchkin baby every now and then. Just try not to overdo it by giving too much and by unintentionally encouraging obesity.

There are a lot of cat treats in stores today, so there's a lot to choose from. Personally, my cats love freeze-dried meat treats, whether they're chicken or beef or tuna. Surprisingly, my munchkin cats also love melons like honeydew and cantaloupe.

Before trying out any treats, though, make sure that you have read the dangerous cats food section above just to be on the safe side. Aside from that, have fun experimenting to see what your munchkin cat will love!

# Chapter 8 – Caring for Your Munchkin Cat and Understanding Its Needs

* * *

You'll be glad to know that munchkin cats are among the most even tempered, congenial, and communicative of cat breeds. Their good nature is so inherent in the breed that finding behavioral problems with a munchkin cat is very rare and is usually a result of a past owner's bad handling of the poor feline. Because of this, munchkin cats and munchkin kittens are easy to satisfy and are generally glad just to spend time with you, even if all its doing is sitting on your lap. That doesn't mean that the munchkin doesn't require a lot of physical interaction and quality time because it does. But it is easily contented; sitting and cuddling or snuggling up to its parent is usually more than enough.

In terms of physical activities, munchkin cats fall in the easy Goldilocks zone of just right. It's not too placid that it hates activities, but it's not overactive either. You won't have to bring your munchkin cat out for long walks, especially since munchkins are generally indoors cats. Its physical needs can be satisfied with a little play time, with cat toys, or with a ball of yarn (remember to put away the yarn in a safe place after playtime). This makes them great companions for kids because they love to play and will join in in just about any game but they will almost never resort to rough play or get angry when teased too much. They are so generally nice that some munchkin cat parents even say that their munchkins get along better with dogs who are goofier and more laid back than some cats who can be competitive and aloof.

Some added notes to consider when caring for your munchkin cat is that they won't take well to being locked in inside a room. Don't keep them behind closed doors so that they don't get restless or uncomfortable. Munchkin cats will feel a strong affection and love for their parents which means that you need to spend time with them and reassure them with your presence. Leaving them alone for too long by themselves is generally not a good idea and will cause some stress for the little feline.

That being said, in cases of danger, a munchkin cat will try its best to defend itself, like any cat or dog would. This will only come into play if it shares the house with other pets that may have behavioral problems or people who may take playing a little too far, to the point of scaring the poor little thing.

In terms of grooming and other maintenance, it all depends on whether you have a munchkin with a short coat or a long coat. Remember, munchkin cats have a varied array of coat length, patterns, and color. That being said, the munchkin cat is generally not a high maintenance breed.

## Grooming Your Munchkin Cat

*Figure 24: A simple wire brush as above is the best tool for grooming your Munchkin Cat.*

Grooming your munchkin cat can be a nice routine that you can have with your little pet. It's a chance to bond and to build trust. That being said, I've often found myself too busy to groom my cats myself, especially since there are currently three of them living with me. Sometimes, the practical thing to do is to have them professionally groomed, and they do love the experience of being primped and polished.

For those times when you can groom your own munchkin cat or for just brushing its coat clean, you'll need the following basic cat grooming tools.

- Nail clippers
- Bristle brush
- Fine tooth comb
- Cat toothbrush or any soft toothbrush and cat toothpaste
- Non-slip rubber mat for bathing
- Towels for just your pet

Whether they have a short coat or long coat, your munchkin cat will need to be brushed regularly, at least once a week, to avoid tangles. If you have a munchkin cat or munchkin kittens that have longer hair, you will need to trim their coat regularly. A coat that's overgrown is more easily tangled, will become dirty faster, and can be uncomfortable for your munchkin whereas regular brushing will keep your cat's coat smooth and clean and it will spread out its natural oils evenly.

The good news is; you can actually shear your munchkin's coat yourself with the right tools. But I personally find trips to have my cats groomed fun. It gives me a chance to look at the new goodies the shop may have for cats, and it's a chance to interact with other cat lovers and to catch up with the latest news and activities within the community.

When it comes to bathing, you will not have to do it as often as you would with a dog or puppy. By nature, cats are extremely fastidious, and your munchkin cat will not be an exception. They will take the time to groom themselves and keep their coats clean. They're so careful about their appearance and hygiene that I would actually recommend you just wash parts of your munchkin cats, the particularly dirty parts or stained parts, instead of a full bath. Most cats just hate baths and will find the experience stressful. That said, there are just times when you can't avoid having to give your cat a bath. Make sure that the process is as enjoyable as possible for the both of you by speaking in soothing tones, by being comforting, and by never resorting to brute force.

When bathing your munchkin cat, it's important that you don't use the shampoo or conditioner for people. Cat shampoo is a lot gentler with no perfumes and will have the right pH level for your little munchkin. If a conditioner isn't needed then don't use it; otherwise, use a special cat conditioner too. You will also need a rubber mat to help keep your munchkin cat from slipping. Don't forget to use warm water, not hot!

Generally, cats will prefer to be dried with a towel instead of a hair dryer because of the noise that a hair dryer can make. If you prefer drying your pets with a hair dryer, you can help your munchkin cat get used to the experience by starting young, as early as when it's still a kitten.

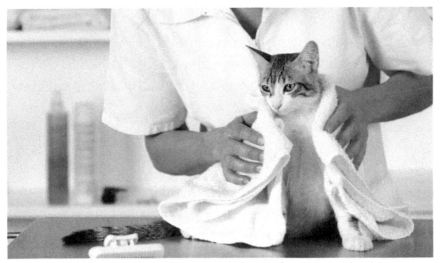

*Figure 25: Towel drying is best after a good bath!*

When choosing a cat shampoo for your munchkin cat, keep in mind that most cats can't stand strong scents. Think twice before you buy that raspberry scented cat shampoo. Instead, go for a more neutral scent and a very gentle shampoo. Also, a lot of shampoos for cats these days surprisingly contain ingredients that are either poisonous to cats or act as irritants.

Here are ingredients that you need to find and avoid in cat shampoos:

Sodium Laureth Sulfide
Cocamide DEA
Peg-40 Lanolin
DMDM Hydantoin
Diazolidinyl Urea
Aloe
Fragrance
Yellow 5 dye

More than bathing your munchkin cat, you will have to trim its claws a lot more frequently. You will need to do this often enough that I would advise you to invest in a cat claw clipper. These usually go for less than $10 / £6 and can last for years if you don't lose it (or if your munchkin cat doesn't hide it away).

Like just about every pet, your munchkin baby will probably feel a little skittish about having its claws trimmed. A good way to get started is to pet your cat, to soothe it until it is comfortable. After it is comfortable on your lap or on the table, take its paw but continue to pet the paw first before trimming. Do this for each paw you trim. It's important that grooming is as enjoyable and stress-free as possible for your munchkin cat so that the next time you have to do it, there won't be a struggle.

When trimming your munchkin cat's claws, it's important to only trim the very tip and as close to a 45° angle as possible. Just like with people, trimming too much of the claws will hurt your munchkin. It will also make trimming its claws in the future next to impossible.

One of the grooming tasks that most cat parents fail to do is brushing their munchkin cat's teeth. Just like us, our feline friends require regular dental care to keep those cavities away. Here's a wake-up call for all cat parents out there - cats that have tooth decay and other dental problems will need a trip to the cat dentist. Your munchkin cat will have to be put under with anesthesia, pain killers, and antibiotics that can cost as much as $900 / £600 if not more. Imagine how much money you can save with a toothbrush and paste kit and use it on your munchkin twice or three times a week.

For your munchkin cat's eyes and ears, you can gently clean them with a damp tissue or towel. Try to remove gunk before it builds up but don't try to reach into the ears as it may cause damage. If you notice that your munchkin is scratching its eyes and ears too much or there is discharge, it's best to pay the vet a visit.

Oh, let's not forget the grooming tool that every cat parent will want and need - a lint roller!

## Giving Your Munchkin Cat Proper Health Care and Maintenance

Before anything else, even before you bring your new munchkin kitten or cat home, you need to make sure that he or she is neutered or spayed or at least make arrangements for it to be done. It is the responsibility of every cat parent to ensure the safety and good health of his or her munchkin cat and all the pets living in their home. If by any chance you are taking your munchkin cat to get neutered or spayed, and you are asked whether you want to have it declawed, I would strongly advise you to say no. Your munchkin cat relies on its claws more than you know, for balance and agility.

If you had your munchkin cat spayed or neutered by a veterinarian, then you already have a good working relationship with a local vet (hopefully), someone who is already familiar with your munchkin baby. Set aside some time to have a conversation with your vet, so that you can cover proper health maintenance for your munchkin as well as preventative medical care. These steps could cover steps as simple as flea and tick prevention to regular visits for check-ups.

If you don't have a vet in mind yet, you can ask for a recommendation from the shelter or the munchkin cat breeder that you got your munchkin cat from. You can also ask other cat parents that you know. It never hurts to find a vet that someone you know and trust already has a positive experience with.

Your vet will walk you through preventive care for your munchkin cat as well as the vaccination shots that your munchkin kitten will need. Some of these shots are required by law, including rabies shots, and booster shots.

To help set your expectations here's what a common vaccination timetable will look like.

| Munchkin Cat/Kitten Age | Step taken | Notes |
|---|---|---|
| 9 weeks old | First injection | |
| 12 weeks old | Second injection | Fully immune and able to go outdoors one week after the second injection. |

| 1 year old | 1st annual booster |
| 2 years old | 2nd annual booster (and so on for every year) |

If you can, ask for a print out of the schedule and stick it on the refrigerator so that you don't forget. Visits to the vet and getting the shots that your munchkin cat needs is crucial so that your pet can live a long and healthy life with you and your family.

Aside from its shots, you need to take steps to prevent any flea or tick problems. Your vet can also recommend medication for this, but a lot of cat parents prefer spot on products - a liquid that you drop onto your munchkin's nape - over flea collars, shampoos, sprays, or flea dust. It's more convenient and a lot more effective, and it doesn't stop you from petting your munchkin cat. While I've used spot on flea prevention products before, I also sometimes use medicine that needs to be added to cat food once a month that stops fleas from reproducing.

Before you use anything on your munchkin cat, I highly recommend that you run everything by your vet first. It's always better to be safe than sorry.

## When Should You Bring Your Munchkin Cat to the Vet

Regular check-ups are all well and good, but it's also important to know when your munchkin cat needs to be taken to the vet for health care. Here are the top ten signs that will tell you to bring your cat to see the pet doctor as soon as possible:

1. When your munchkin cat changes its behavior and starts to urinate or defecate outside of the litter box.
2. When your munchkin suddenly shies away from attention or from socializing with other pets or people.
3. When your munchkin cat suddenly becomes too inactive throughout the day.
4. When your munchkin cat stops eating or drinking water.
5. When your munchkin cat loses weight suddenly and inexplicably.
6. When it changes its grooming habits and starts to 'let go'.
7. When your munchkin cat has bad breath.
8. When your munchkin cat has discharge in its orifices, like its eyes, ears, or nose.
9. When your munchkin's urine shows signs of blood.
10. When your munchkin cat is suffering from an ingrown paw nail.

# Chapter 9 – Can You Train A Munchkin Cat?

* * *

The answer is yes! Munchkin cats are very intelligent, responsive, and communicative. When it comes to following the house rules, you won't really have to lift a finger when it comes to cats, especially munchkins. All you have to do is set up the litter box, and they will know that it's their designated toilet. They will know when they are going to be fed if you stick to a routine and reinforce it. They are the epitome of low maintenance and independent. So let's forget teaching your munchkin cat the house rules for a second and think about teaching them a few fun tricks!

The important thing to remember is that something as fun-loving and friendly as your munchkin cat won't respond to negative reinforcement, but you can do miracles with simple praise, petting, and some yummy treats. Your munchkin will need something special to motivate it so try to keep an eye out for the treats that it particularly loves and use it to your advantage. In my case, dried meat treats have always worked wonders.

Let's start with a few basic tricks for beginners to help you get the hang of communicating with your cat. If you want to invest in teaching your cats how to do tricks more, you can buy a clicker to help get its attention.

Pro Tip!

Don't want to buy a clicker for
munchkin cat training? Use a click
pen instead!

**Teach Your Munchkin Cat to Sit On Command**

*Figure 26: As strange as it may seem, Munchkin Cats
are just as trainable as most dogs!*

Just like dogs, cats can learn how to sit on command when properly motivated and it's very easy. The first thing to do is to separate your munchkin from anything distracting. You will never get anything done when its attention is divided by the television, the fish in the aquarium, or your kids! Bring the little munchkin to a room where it's just the two of you so that you'll have its undivided attention.

Get your munchkin cat's attention by giving them a small taste of the treats you have for it. Be warned, your munchkin will definitely try to bully you into giving it more treats. Do not give in! Instead, firmly call its attention away from the treats in your hand. If you have a clicker, use it to get your cat's attention.

The next step is to firmly tell your cat to sit using the command word 'sit.' At this point, your cat will have no idea what you mean. If it sits, it's just a coincidence. Praise and pet it anyway and give it a well-deserved treat.

After you've familiarized your munchkin cat with the word 'sit', take it further by gently placing your cat into a sitting position. Once its butt touches the ground, say the word 'sit' again. Then praise it and offer a treat. Repeat this a few more times until your cat responds to the command word. Your munchkin cat being a munchkin, it should catch on pretty quick.

After a while, you can wean your munchkin cat away from treats by using the clicker more and more.

## Teach Your Munchkin Cat to Come on Command

This is probably the easiest trick in the book. I teach my cats how to come on command by making a distinct sound before placing their food in their dishes or when their food is ready. It's usually just a whistle, and because I whistle pretty badly, it's very distinct. After a few meals, they learn to come when I whistle. Easy as pie.

You can substitute my whistle with the word 'come'. Try to let your munchkin cat get used to hearing the word before feedings, then try using the command word in a completely different setting, like when you're in the living room reading. When your munchkin cat responds to the command word and comes over, shower it with praise and give it a delicious treat.

Repeat this regularly, eventually replacing the treats with just petting or the clicker just to continue reinforcing the trick.

## How to Train Your Munchkin Cat to Use the Toilet

This is a lot tougher to train on purpose, but I did have a cat once that caught right on. This kitten's name was Carla, and I found her when she was a tiny little thing, abandoned right on my doorstep. She eventually became part of the family and, because she never grew up with other cats and we didn't have any at the time, she became mimicking us instead. One day, I saw her climb onto the toilet and start pooping. I didn't disturb her, just watched from afar. After she was done, she turned around, pushed the flush lever down, and daintily left the premises. After a while, I put the litter box away. We can't all be so lucky as to run into a cat as quick on the uptake as my Carla but your munchkin cat is certified smart and will be easier to train than most cats.

This trick will take more time than the others, but it will definitely be convenient on your part. The first step is to place the litter box beside the toilet, slowly placing it closer and closer to the toilet every day. Eventually, you will need to raise it higher and higher too, until it is on the same level as the toilet. Once your munchkin cat has gotten used to using the litter box this way, you will need to transition to a special kind of litter box that fits over the toilet. You will be using flushable litter.

Once it is used to the new litter box, you can gradually reduce the litter that you use, letting your munchkin grow accustomed to not needing it. When it is completely used to the new setup, remove the litter box from the toilet. Eventually, it will be using your toilet like a pro.

This trick can be pretty cool, but I would also advise caution, especially for a munchkin cat. Given its small size, your cat could fall into the toilet and have trouble getting out. If you are going to try this trick, don't use any chemicals for the toilet water, like toilet cleaners. This is poisonous to most living things, including your beloved munchkin cat.

*Figure 27: Yes, it CAN be done!*

## Use Treats and Training to Reinforce Good Behavior

More than just teaching your munchkin cat how to do a few
neat tricks, you can use the same reward system to
reinforce good behavior and to put a stop to bad behavior.
In the case of a munchkin cat, you can encourage your pet
to stop climbing onto the high shelves to keep it from
getting into any painful accidents or from breaking any
vases. You can also dissuade it from climbing onto the
window screens. Your munchkin cat can just as easily
explore other parts of the house or express its pent up
energy somewhere else, in places less dangerous or risky.

As for teaching your cats newer tricks, the sky is actually
the limit. You can teach your munchkin cat how to shake
paws with you, how to beg (though this looks weird on
cats), how to walk on a leash, anything! Just use your treats
or your clicker wisely and pour out the praise. Your cat will
love the attention.

# Chapter 10 – Munchkin Cat Groups, and Other Fun Activities

*  *  *

One of the best ways to enjoy your munchkin cat's company is to socialize within the munchkin cat community. This could mean finding other munchkin cat parents just so you can have someone to discuss your pet with, to join groups that specialize in munchkins, or to sign up for online communities where you can get information and share pictures of your munchkin cat.

Some groups include all munchkin cats while other groups are exclusive to mixes like the Scottish fold munchkin, the Persian munchkin, the Lambkin and other crosses. From my experience, most groups are very friendly and glad to meet anyone who shares their interests in cats and love for munchkins in particular. They are also great for getting inside information, like which places are friendly to cats for vacations or outdoor activities.

Want to know where to get started? Facebook, Flickr, and Pinterest are good places to look. In Flickr, there are photography groups that you can join where you can see pictures of other people's munchkins and add some of your own. It can be a lot of fun, and it's all very interactive. And let's face it; the online cat community is very, very strong and can offer endless adorable pictures!

You can also keep an eye out for any cat activities in the local scene, or you can make the trip to some big cat festivals like the Edmonton International Cat Festival held in Canada. Most of the proceeds from this event goes to various charities, so you're helping out and enjoying yourself too.

In the US, you can also mark your calendars for the yearly Love Your Pet Expo that has events ranging from photography contests and costume contests to AKC CGC testing. In the UK, some of the popular cat events include running events and challenge events to help raise money for cats and kittens, free veterinary webinars, and the GCCF Supreme Cat Show that is held every year for all cat lovers!

The UK's GCCF Supreme Cat Show is a favorite in the parent cat community. Its events include competitions and exhibitions, a 'meet the cat' program where you can get to know your favorite cat breed better, plus lots of stands selling goodies!

Don't have a munchkin cat or cat group in your community? Why not consider starting one? Even just a small group of friends can offer a great outlet for talking about all things munchkin. Personally, I enjoy having friends who also love cats to talk to, someone I can exchange notes with or call when I feel my cat is sick. These are also the people to call when you plan on going on vacation, and you need someone to cat sit. With cats of their own, they are more than prepared to deal with your munchkin baby for a short amount of time. Plus, they would usually love to have a friendly munchkin cat over, especially since munchkins get along so well with others.

## Try Going on a Munchkin Cat Vacation

*Figure 28: This Munchkin Cat seems to be wanting to go to Russia, but it's best you make the travel decisions!*

Speaking of vacations, why not consider going on a munchkin cat vacation with your pet instead of leaving it with friends? As cats become more and more part of our everyday lives and core families, a lot of cat parents are hesitant to leave their pets behind even for just the span of a vacation. After all, the family doesn't feel as complete without our friendly felines.

Thankfully, more and more hotels are accommodating when it comes to cat guests, and munchkin cats are even less of a problem, with their easy to placate and friendly nature. For your next vacation, why not try bringing your munchkin along?

Here are some cat-friendly destinations and accommodations for you.

### 1. The Queen Mary 2

You can visit their website at http://www.cunard.com/

Yes, the Cunard cruise line has a cat-friendly ship that will treat your munchkin cat with its own feline vacation while you enjoy yourself. They will have spacious kennels, play areas, fleece blankets, toys, and treats and you can visit them as much as you want.

If you've been thinking about going on a cruise but you don't want to leave your munchkin behind, the Queen Mary 2 should offer a great experience for the both of you.

### 2. The Kimpton Hotels

You can visit their website at https://www.kimptonhotels.com/

There are cat-friendly hotels, and then there are cat-friendly hotels. At the Kimpton Hotels, your baby munchkin cat will be greeted by name as is fit for your VIP cat. Your room will also be decked out for your munchkin's comfort as well as yours. Think scratch posts and a plush bed.

Want to enjoy activities with your munchkin cat? You can indulge in wine tasting with your feline date. They even have an in-room pet massage so you can both relax and de-stress together. I kid you not.

### 3. Hotel Monteleone in New Orleans

You can visit their website at http://hotelmonteleone.com/

This cat-friendly hotel is located in the popular French quarter and will offer a lot of comforts that any self-respecting munchkin cat will expect. Your pet will enjoy monogrammed food and water bowls, gourmet treats, and even floors that are completely cat-friendly which means that your munchkin will be free to stroll, to explore, and to meet new cat friends! Your munchkin might even enjoy this hotel more than you.

# Chapter 11 – Living Happily with Your Munchkin Cat

\* \* \*

Having a cat – especially a cat that's as special and as adorable as a munchkin cat – can be a very fulfilling experience. When you commit to bringing a munchkin cat or munchkin kitten into your family, you are making a lifelong commitment that will keep on bringing joy into your life. And the more your bond grows with your munchkin, the more easily you can communicate with each other and get a feel for the other's emotions. I've had some of my cats for more than a decade, and I could always tell when one of them wasn't feeling well or was in trouble or had simply been naughty. In return, they recognized my moods. If I felt sad one morning, my cats would always be a step behind me and would grab the chance to snuggle with me and be cuddled. I cared for them and loved them, and they responded by being caring and loving as well.

Munchkin cats, like all pets, are bright, responsive creatures and how they grow up all depends on the way they are treated by their cat parents. A munchkin cat that has been cared for and cuddled and properly trained towards good behavior can be a real joy to have in your home. You can come home to a munchkin that's genuinely pleased to see you and offers to play if you have time. Sometimes those simple things can brighten up a bad day or add joy to an already good one. And munchkin cats and munchkin kittens are the perfect breed for affection and play.

With this book on munchkin cats and how to raise them and care for them, you are better prepared than most cat parents. The fact that you took the time to read this book shows how invested you are in raising your munchkin cat right and taking responsibility as a cat parent. That is an excellent start for setting the groundwork. And believe me, you will reap the benefits in the long run. But more than just making sure your cat is fed and watered and plays well with others, you also want to provide a loving and affectionate home for this sensitive feline soul. After all, munchkin cats are more sociable than most breeds and will thrive with communication and attention.

As a last minute reminder to spend time and have fun with your new munchkin cat, here are some fun activities that you can do together, ways to create a playful environment for your munchkin, and maybe a couple of ways to spoil your short-legged cat a little.

## 1. Walk your cat on a leash.

Munchkin cats only need moderate exercise so walking it on a leash isn't really a necessity. Instead, it's more of a fun activity that will get the both of you outdoors. Not all cats will take to being walked on a leash though, so it's better to start them young. You can also use the reward system that we used in the chapter for training your munchkin cat by offering a treat or using a clicker to reinforce good behavior.

If you do want to spend time outdoors with your munchkin cat, it is important to have it on a leash for safety. You don't want your pet to wander away or worse, to get too close to another pet that may not be as gentle or good-natured.

## 2. Get some toys.

There are plenty of toys that you and your munchkin can have fun with. A simple laser will do for a game of chase the light, but you can also get wand toys with something at the end, bouncy rubber balls, and catnip toys.

My cats' favorite toys include a treat maze, a cat wand with a squeaky mouse toy, a foam soccer ball and a ball of yarn. Like any responsible cat parent, I make sure to put away their toys, especially the ball of yarn, when we're done playing.

Don't overdo it with the laser pointer though or your cat may get a little too frustrated and even upset.

## 3. Offer perches by the windows.

I would always recommend that you keep your cat indoors because it can be dangerous for them to wander outdoors. That doesn't mean that you can't create some interactive ways for your dwarf cat or dwarf kitten to enjoy the outdoors inside your home.

You can offer perches by the window so that they can peek outside anytime you want. Add some bird houses outside your window or a feeding station for squirrels and your munchkin cat can enjoy watching other furred creatures visiting the house.

## 4. Put cat grass around the house.

*Figure 29: High Fiber diets aren't just for people!*

Having containers of cat grass in your home hits two birds with one stone. It gives your munchkin cat a dose of the outdoors while also giving it a chance to digest the grass which, unlike catnip, doesn't give cats a high but does help with digestion and some nutrients that they're missing from their diet.

## 5. Buy or build a cat tree.

A cat tree is made up of layers of perches that your munchkin cat can climb onto and explore. Some of the perches can have parts that your munchkin can scratch while others may have toys dangling for your it to play with. It can be a lot of fun and very easy to build. If you're not too handy with a hammer, you can also find these cat trees at pet supply stores. It doesn't hurt to spoil your munchkin cat a little.

## 6. Buy a cat bed.

It never hurts to set aside a corner or an area for your munchkin cat, given every cat's territorial nature. But as every cat parent will tell you, nothing is stopping your cat from claiming any area of the house as their own. One of my cats took a liking to my favorite chair in the living room, and it has been an endless battle of who gets there first ever since. Still, it doesn't hurt to indulge yourself a little and try to dissuade your short-legged cat friend from declaring your favorite spot as feline property.

There are plenty of other things that you can do with your cat or other items that can help make your home just as much your munchkin cat's home. In time, you'll find endless options, and you'll be surprised at the things that you'll learn just by meeting more people who also have munchkins. These are all things that will come naturally as a cat parent.

*Figure 30: Ever eager & playful, the Munchkin Cat makes a great companion.*

For now, I recommend that you enjoy your munchkin cat's company, get to know each other, and learn each other's habits. Trust me when I say that it can be a very fulfilling relationship and that you won't regret bringing home this short-legged cat as a family and friend. And who knows, maybe after spending a few years with your munchkin cat, you'll open your home to one or two more.

**Final Thoughts on Your Journey with Your Munchkin Cat**

The best thing about bringing home a munchkin cat is having a lifelong friend, someone to come home to every day, and someone to play with and interact with whether you live alone, or you're with your partner and kids. The more you get to know your munchkin, the more you'll find that it has its own distinct personality complete with dislikes and favorites and you'll learn to understand your pet the same way you would form a relationship with a human being. And as your relationship grows, your munchkin cat will learn to understand you too.

I have had a lot of cats live with me over the years, some of them munchkins and some of them not, but every single one of them grew to become important members of the family. We traveled with them; we spent the holidays with them, and they returned the favor by being loving and affectionate pets. My children grew up with cats (and sometimes dogs) in the household, and they learned how to care for smaller beings that were fragile and sensitive, and I think they grew up to be gentler and stronger because of it.

At the end of this book, I can only hope that you learned as much as I wanted to impart and that you find your relationship with your munchkin cat or munchkin kitten as fulfilling as mine has been with my own pets. I wish you and your new pet and family member the best of luck!

CPSIA information can be obtained
at www.ICGtesting.com
Printed in the USA
LVOW06s1447291216
519134LV00032B/203/P

9 781911 355007